PEYAKOW

PEYAKOW

RECLAIMING CREE DIGNITY

Darrel J. McLeod

MILKWEED EDITIONS

Published 2021 by Milkweed Editions
Printed in the United States of America
Cover design by Mary Austin Speaker
Cover photo by Ilja Herb; cover illustration by Mary Austin Speaker
21 22 23 24 25   5 4 3 2 1
First Edition

Milkweed Editions, an independent nonprofit publisher, gratefully acknowledges sustaining support from the Alan B. Slifka Foundation and its president, Riva Ariella Ritvo-Slifka; the Ballard Spahr Foundation; *Copper Nickel*; the Jerome Foundation; the McKnight Foundation; the National Endowment for the Arts; the National Poetry Series; the Target Foundation; and other generous contributions from foundations, corporations, and individuals. Also, this activity is made possible by the voters of Minnesota through a Minnesota State Arts Board Operating Support grant, thanks to a legislative appropriation from the arts and cultural heritage fund. For a full listing of Milkweed Editions supporters, please visit milkweed.org.

Library of Congress Cataloging-in-Publication Data

Names: McLeod, Darrel J., author.
Title: Peyakow : reclaiming Cree dignity / Darrel McLeod.
Other titles: Reclaiming Cree dignity
Description: First edition. | Minneapolis, Minnesota : Milkweed Editions, 2021. |
Summary: "Following his debut memoir, Mamaskatch, which masterfully portrayed a Cree coming-of-age in rural Canada, Darrel J. McLeod continues the poignant story of his adulthood in Peyakow"--Provided by publisher.
Identifiers: LCCN 2021016611 (print) | LCCN 2021016612 (ebook) | ISBN 9781571313973 (paperback) | ISBN 9781571317438 (ebook)
Subjects: LCSH: McLeod, Darrel J. | Cree Indians--Biography. | McLeod, Darrel J.--Family. | Canada. Indian and Northern Affairs Canada--Officials and employees--Biography. | Indigenous peoples--Canada--Government relations. | Indigenous peoples--Canada--Land tenure. | Indigenous men--Canada--Biography. | Indian gays--Canada--Biography. | Two-spirit people--Canada--Biography.
Classification: LCC E99.C88 M348 2021 (print) | LCC E99.C88 (ebook) | DDC 971.2004/973230092 [B]--dc23
LC record available at https://lccn.loc.gov/2021016611
LC ebook record available at https://lccn.loc.gov/2021016612

Milkweed Editions is committed to ecological stewardship. We strive to align our book production practices with this principle, and to reduce the impact of our operations in the environment. We are a member of the Green Press Initiative, a nonprofit coalition of publishers, manufacturers, and authors working to protect the world's endangered forests and conserve natural resources. *Peyakow* was printed on acid-free 100% postconsumer-waste paper by McNaughton-Gunn.

Love is something that you can leave behind
you when you die—it is that powerful.

—JOHN FIRE LAME DEER (1903–76),
LAKOTA HOLY MAN

Darrel James McLeod—Lapatak—*isiyegaso*. Slave Lake *ohci niya*. Bertha Dora *nigawi*, Clifford James (Sonny) *notawiy*.

I've been living in exile from my homeland for over five decades, separated from my people, my culture and language, the rivers and streams, hunting grounds and berry patches—the entire ecosystem of which I am a part; an ecosystem that has been permanently altered. I can never recuperate the pristine creek we used to drink from; its life-giving water nurtured my nascent being. I can never revisit the idyllic meadows where as children countless cousins and I frolicked worry free from dawn to dusk in the territory where the spirits of our ancestors dwell to this day, a land now traversed by pipelines and penetrated by compressor stations and pumpjacks.

The birds—our constant companions and allies—have diminished in number. The monarch butterflies had all but disappeared but seem to be making a comeback. And the water level of the rivers has gone down by approximately one-third.

After laborious research and deep reflection over the last few years, I now grasp how my extended family, once proud and strong, independent and thriving, became disenfranchised and impoverished while the society around us grew increasingly affluent. In the pages of this book, I write what I've come to understand about the colonization of my people and tell the story of how I struggled to turn around our dystopian lives, striving to salvage some degree of happiness and well-being not only for myself and my family but also for Indigenous individuals and peoples in Canada and other parts of the world.

saweyimik kahkiyaw nitôtêminânak mîna niwâhkômâkaninânak

Contents

Miyoskamin

SKIPEW—THE WATER WAS up to there. The reedy plains near the mouth of *Ayahciniyiw sîpîy*, the Slave River, were submersed, the confluent streams high. Widespread flooding was still possible. The ice barrage, with its monstrous, angular protrusions, had broken into boulder-sized chunks that floated steadily downstream, diminishing in size as they moved.

Miyoskamin was well underway. The frozen quiet of winter had gradually melted into a symphony: the chirps, twitters and whistling of song sparrows—their looped call and response providing a backdrop to the trilled oboe call of loons. The *ek ek ek ek* of magpies and the staccato drumming of a woodpecker beckoning its life mate. Pussy willows became catkins, gradually giving way to untried leaves.

Joseph watched as a mini-iceberg drifted past, bobbing and shifting in the middle of the river where the current was swiftest. At sixteen, he was an astute paddler who understood the danger these glacial remnants represented for scows or canoes. Only about a third of the ice mass was above the agitated water; the bulk of it lurked below the surface, and if your boat struck that part, it was all over—everything was lost and anyone in the boat would surely drown. Joseph had had a few close calls. Boat, horseback or dogsled—those were the three ways to get to his territory, situated around Lesser Slave Lake—*Ayahciniyiw saakahikan.*

After two weeks of torrential rain, the turquoise sky was vast and calm, but Joseph knew this wouldn't last. Before the rainy weather set in, his family had survived a violent windstorm. He and his closest cousins had been out on the land scouting for gooseberries when a sudden silence fell. The birds had hushed and the animals had taken cover in their dens, or wherever they could find it. The young Nehiyawak froze where they stood. Within minutes, the wind whipped up, bending tall aspen trees over as if they were tender willows, snapping some off at the top. Joseph had ducked into a copse of tamarack trees to avoid flying branches and debris, motioning for his cousins to follow him.

"*Astamitik, kwee ah hu,*" he yelled.

Now, as *miyoskamin* unfolded, more *Moniyawak* appeared on the river, using oars, poles, small sails or some combination of these in their quest to find treasure. Even a haul of a few small gold nuggets seemed worthwhile to them. What joy could a lump of cold shiny metal bring to anyone? The Nehiyaw elders were troubled by the increasing presence of the blond strangers, and Joseph was too.

Most of these prospectors didn't bother to wave to Joseph and his cousins as they passed by in their scows, let alone come ashore to make the acquaintance of his parents or grandparents. It was always a surprise when one of them stopped in, hoping to trade whatever they could for *mosoyas*—steaks, roasts or ribs, maybe even some of the prized moose jerky the Nehiyawak called *kakiwak*—or pemmican, a mixture of powdered *kakiwak*, grease and dried berries. *Wapus* that tasted like chicken, its roasted elongated ears crunchy and flavourful. Tobacco and tea.

Those prospectors who did visit, always men, sought out the company of women, or of men who dressed and acted like women. Some tried to lure younger boys with offers of candy. The pale, bearded strangers had bad breath and a putrid body odour. They were pushy—frenetic—anxious to get rich, if not with gold, then with oil. Unlike the *Mistikisiwak*, the French-speaking fur traders who came and went in canoes, the prospectors had no interest in learning Nehiyaw. These men would not co-operate or attempt to fit in—they wanted absolute control, nothing less.

Joseph was relieved that the wayfarers had only ever asked him to help fasten or load their boats in exchange for a coin or two—no attempts at touching. Some of his younger friends had given in to curiosity or to the desire for sweets. Those boys later recounted the unpleasant intimacy with the white strangers—it wasn't electrically charged exhilaration like their precocious play with each other.

What the newcomers couldn't acquire by bartering, they attempted to take by force. Between their stubbornness, their money and their weapons, nothing, it seemed, could stop them. Stories of bloody confrontations, sometimes resulting in the death of one or more Nehiyawak, travelled up and down the river—the moccasin telegraph.

Kihci-môhkomâwa, Joseph's father had called these white men, because of the long knives attached to the rifles of their soldiers. They called themselves "h'Americuns." Joseph recalled the stories he'd heard about wars between the *Kihci-môhkomâwa* and the tribes to the south. His people still talked about a brutal war the *Kihci-môhkomâwa* had waged nearby, across the mountains, when Joseph's father was a young man. They had arrived unexpectedly with a group of armed warriors. They raped women and girls, torched villages and destroyed precious salmon grounds— diverting streams and rivulets while digging for gold.

One afternoon, during a break in the rain, Joseph was astonished to see a scow trekking up the river carrying three *Kaskitewiyasak*. They paddled to the docks, tied their boat and came ashore. A crowd of Joseph's family and friends gathered, fascinated to see these people they'd only heard rumours of—smooth skin blacker than Joseph's darkest *cucuum*, tall and strong.

It took some time for these sojourners to communicate that they weren't prospecting for gold. They were scouting a place for their families to settle. Through a blend of hand gestures, words and drawings on the ground, the *Kaskitewiyasak* explained that they'd travelled from the far south.

"*Maci manitowi Kihci-môhkomâwa*," Joseph's father said to the dark men once he grasped what they were trying to convey. A couple of hours after their arrival, the three black men sat around a campfire, interacting with Joseph's parents in a way that was more like a guessing game than a conversation. They chewed dry meat and bit into chunks of bannock slathered with pemmican, washing it all down with wild mint tea.

Without warning, a small group of armed white men appeared. One of them began shouting at the dark-skinned visitors. Joseph listened carefully and watched the repeated sweeping gestures of the man's free hand—his index finger jabbing toward the boat of the *Kaskitewiyasak* while he vehemently yelled something over and over.

"*Wah wah pakwâsowewin*," Joseph muttered.

His parents nodded. "*Tapwe-ci*."

Using his rifle, one of the *Moniyawak* motioned for the visitors to go back to their skiff. The dark men gathered up their few belongings, along with the packets of dried meat and mint tea Joseph's father had gifted them, and hastened toward their boat. The air was thick with bitterness. Why this lethal hatred? Joseph wondered.

Joseph liked to sit around the fire in the evening to listen to the elders and community leaders talking. The quest for gold and oil was bringing more *Kihci-môhkomâwa* north. Armed conflict, the type they'd heard about in the south and just across the mountains, hung in the air, so something had to be done. The Nehiyawak had demanded a treaty, but with better terms than those the new "government" had imposed on their southern relatives and the *Ayahciniyiw*, their historical enemy. They did not want their hunting restricted to certain areas—they wanted to continue hunting far and wide, as they always had. They would demand education for their children as well as other important concessions in exchange for allowing the h'Americuns peaceful access to their territory in a sharing of use and occupation type of arrangement.

One day word arrived that finally the government was sending a delegation upriver. They were also sending gendarmes—*simaganisak*—to keep the peace. This was the first real sign of the Canadian government's presence since they claimed to have purchased Nehiyaw territory, and all the territory around it, from the Hudson's Bay Company.

A half-breed factor from that company had tried to describe the British royalty to Joseph in Cree one day, along with their system of land ownership or title. Afterwards, Joseph had repeated the story to friends and family, only to be mocked. How could a great white mother own the entire Nehiyaw world and beyond?

❖

Word had arrived during the winter months that the new government required the Nehiyawak to select chiefs. The message had recently been repeated, for it was now urgent to do so—these chiefs would negotiate with the government representatives who were en route to decide the future of Joseph's people. And even though it wasn't their custom, Joseph's extended family and the other Nehiyawak from around the lake selected four men to lead their side of the talks.

During three weeks of persistent spring rain, the four leaders convened around a campfire daily. Joseph sat nearby, drawn in by the intensity of their conversation. Each day the medicine men led the four leaders in ceremony to seek clarity and wisdom. In the evenings, often late into the night, everyone in the camp played games and told stories to uproarious laughter.

Today the chiefs' faces were dour. Each in turn spoke about the conclusions they had reached in discussion with their wives to clarify their strategy and approach.

"We have to be cunning to get the best deal we can." Giroux was always the most practical. "Mistahe Muskwa—Big Bear—was one of the greatest Nehiyaw chiefs from the south, and look what they did to him when he resisted—starved out his tribe, cut off his hair, accused him of betraying the great white mother and put him in jail. He died a year after they let him go."

"Their medicine is potent," Neesotasis said. "My *iskwew* says their *manitou* is three in one—*notawiy, napesis, mina gitchi manitou*—Father, Son and Holy Ghost. And they eat human flesh—the flesh of the son of their *manitou*. In their ceremonies they convert a piece of bread into His body. And they drink His blood from a shiny metal cup."

Joseph felt acid rush to his throat. Didn't the white men know anyone who ate human flesh became a *wihtikiw*? Were they all *wihtikiwak*?

The four leaders continued their conversation.

"Their medicine men deny their own needs—claim that these urges for *masiwêwin* are seeded by a *maci manitou*. But the *Mistikisiwak* tell us that the black robes do go with women—they just lie about it.

"Yes, like the story about the young black robe transporting the body of a teen Nehiyaw girl who had died while away from home back to her family's camp to be buried among her people. Some Nehiyawak came upon him in the forest halfway through his journey, on top of the girl's corpse, grinding and moaning. When the incensed men asked him what he was doing, he said the girl was a devil, that she'd caused him to fall into her coffin. *Wah wah sosquats.* If he hadn't been a black robe, the men would've beaten him. Instead they left him to the mercy of his own *manitou.*"

"They say their leader was chosen by their *manitou.* They call her 'queen' and say she owns this land. Is she human or a spirit? They talk like she is human."

"How can they say anyone owns the earth—the land, the wind, water and fire—the animals? They can only belong to *Kitse Manitou.*"

"*Mah*, and they don't give anything back. Just take and take. When our great leaders accumulate wealth, they give it all back to the people. That is our way. But not them."

The four leaders fell quiet, contemplating the shrinking ice floe on the river. A cool breeze had displaced the warm air currents of the day before.

Kinoosayoo broke the silence. "Ever since those *Moniyawak* stole *Manito Asiniy*, our power has diminished. That rock fell from the sky at the beginning of time. It has protected us and our relations on the plains. Now we have no protection against the *manitowi* they bring."

Moostos spoke. "Yes, and they spread disease. Instead of burning the clothing and blankets of their dead, they distribute those possessions to Nehiyawak as gifts. So many of our people have died. Entire villages have perished. One of the *Kihci-môhkomâwa* said some *Moniyawak* around here have *maskihkîy* to keep people from catching the disease and have had it for years but they don't use it."

"*Scanak kosanak*! They have watched our people die—ours and those from many tribes that we traded with—the Dakelh, the Tŝilhqot'in, the Okanagan, the Nisga'a and beyond, as far as the big salty lake. The *Moniyawak* spread diseases that they themselves have carried to our lands."

"Some of our young warriors want to kill these white people when they arrive to send a message to their queen that we won't give up our freedom."

"Killing them will only bring more. And they'll bring *simaganisak* with rifles and long knives. More will follow. They come on large ships from their faraway land. We have to control our young men. But if the *Moniyawak* start to kill our people with guns, the way they have in the south, then we'll need fiery warriors."

"*Tapwe.* They execute all who resist. Remember what happened to those chiefs across the mountains, the ones who call themselves Tŝilhqot'in, who warred to protect their territory and rivers. The government men tricked six chiefs into going to their camp for a meeting, then hanged them. All within a couple of days. Just for protecting their territory."

"Yes, and what about the *Apihtawikosisan* leader, Louis Riel? Even got himself elected into their government. They still hanged him."

"In some places they send their whisky sellers in. Some of our people will do anything to get their hands on *iskotewapoy*—sell their furs really cheap, even sell their lodges and supplies."

"*Sosquats maci manitowi.* Let's kill them the way we've killed our other enemies."

"No. The *Moniyawak* have horses and gunpowder. More lethal diseases. Our medicine men say the *Moniyawak* will dominate for ten generations, then their greed and selfishness will ruin them. We'll regain our strength. But for now, we'll work out the best deal we can."

"They'll divide us. Already, they've told us we must choose four chiefs to meet with them. We won't know what their papers say. Peokus can talk their language, but he can't read it. They're offering to make us richer than the rest of our people. And there is no *sohkiskâkewin,* no chance for us to bring the treaty document to our people and seek their agreement."

"Many of our people already left. They know what's coming."

"The *Moniyawak* haven't kept their promises with our relations to the south. Why would they keep their word to us? We Nehiyawak already have everything we need. We live long and travel freely—send hunting parties as far as the mountains. We trade with the tribes around us. The crazy *Kihci-môhkomâwa* h'Americuns who canoe up and down the river are a threat, but this will pass."

"*Tapwe,* our medicine carriers have stalled them as long as they could. The government men will probably be travelling with their most powerful black robes. Birds carry messages of warning, and animal numbers are dwindling: beaver, moose, deer, muskrat, mink and even wolves. Farther south, the buffalo have all but disappeared."

❖

Joseph jumped up as a boy darted into the encampment, yelling, "They're here… the *Moniyawak* in their boats. The old guide is with them. *Mina* black robe and *simaganisak* with long guns."

Joseph rushed to the docks just in time to see an old priest rise in the scow shakily and make the sign of the cross while mumbling something. The guide and translator everyone knew as Peokus was the first one off the boat. He stepped toward Joseph.

"*Tansi?*"

"*Key'ops ekosi.*"

Some of the local *Moniyawak* came to meet the delegation and help them set up. A large canvas tent in the middle would serve as a meeting place. After the *Moniyawak* had settled in, made a fire, prepared a simple meal and eaten, the old black robe, Père Lacombe, tried to usher everyone into the tent.

As soon as he entered, Joseph knew what was going on—he'd seen a black robe lead a ceremony before. The only thing similar to the ceremonies of his people was the smoke the priest wafted around the tent by swinging a shiny basket hanging from a chain. The smell gave Joseph shivers. Did the black robes want to replace sweetgrass, sage and tree fungus with this new herb they were burning? Was their smudge more powerful?

That evening, the medicine men called all the Nehiyaw men to a pipe ceremony. In a clearing slightly removed from the camp they chanted, passed a pipe around and danced well into the night. In the sky above, the wispy spirits performed their own ritual to the call-and-answer howling of wolves and coyotes and the screeches of owls. When Joseph finally made it to his cot, he was vibrating.

Joseph didn't understand the lilting English of the white headman's speech the next day. The Cree-sounding words that came out of the puffy pink lips of the young red-headed translator didn't make sense to him either. He could decipher three terms: *kâkike*, *kihcôkimâw* and *kahkiya kîkway*. These words were repeated so often that Joseph made the connection with the matching English terms: "forever," "king" and "everything." Joseph came to life when Kinoosayoo launched into a speech in fast-paced Cree, stumping the translator.

"Our ceremonies will not stop—not even while you're here among us, but we know about your law, and some of our people already practise our ceremonies in secret. We shouldn't have to hide this. And we cannot be restricted in our hunting. We must be able to move freely every summer to get our winter supply of meat, berries, plants and medicines. Without this we will not agree."

To demonstrate their support for the four chiefs, all the Nehiyawak in the tent stood to leave.

Black Robe himself stood, struck a dramatic pose and spoke. In his broken Cree he assured the Nehiyawak that the lead commissioner was a man of God and would not deceive anyone. The Nehiyawak would be able to carry on with their lives as before, except that in the future they would share the territory with white men and they would have some lands set aside just for them.

That night Joseph joined the others in a sweat lodge ceremony. As soon as he got to his bed he fell into a deep sleep. He awoke just after sunrise and crept outside, summoned by songbirds.

Joseph ambled to a boulder near the shore and perched on it. This was his favourite place to observe the river. To his surprise he spied a young Nehiyaw man paddling toward the dock. The young man stepped out of his canoe adroitly and strode over to where Joseph sat. When he reached out, Joseph reluctantly extended his hand. The young Nehiyaw brought his other hand forward to pat the back of Joseph's.

"*Tansi*, Mosom. *Miyokisikow*," he said.

Joseph drew back. This young man looked familiar, but who could he be? Young Nehiyawak often called each other *Mosom*—Grandfather—in jest, as a term of affection, but this didn't seem to be what was happening now. Suddenly, words just came out of Joseph's mouth. "*Tapwe nisîmis. Miyokisikow.*" Why had he called this man younger brother?

The strange young man continued to address Joseph in Cree.

"We're headed for trying times, Mosom. Our people. It will continue for seven generations, and our family will suffer deeply. Our language, our culture, our very existence will be endangered. Mosom, our family needs you to stay strong, to show us how to survive."

The young man reached into his coat pocket and took out a shiny metal disc. With his thumb, he flipped the disc open to reveal a dial with two small pointy arms, one longer than the other. The youth gently rotated the miniscule wheel attached to the disc between his thumb and index finger. He explained to Joseph that the wheel kept the device working, and it had to be wound twice a day. He described to Joseph its purpose—to measure seconds, minutes and hours. The months, years and centuries would take care of themselves.

The strange young man closed the silver disc and folded it into Joseph's hand. Then the man pulled his shoulders back and stood tall. "*Ekosi maga* Mosom. *Kitwam kawapumitin.*" With this, he pivoted toward his canoe. Halfway there, the young man hesitated, then turned and stepped back toward Joseph, handing him something from his shoulder bag. It was a crimson heart-shaped orb with a sudden delicate fragrance. "Taste it—it's sweet," the young man said.

Joseph was glad the young man had turned back one last time. He had considered calling him back, but what name would he have used? He reached down for the eagle feather from his medicine bundle, offering it to the young man. The stranger cradled the feather close to his heart as he strode back toward the river.

❖

A Note on Treaty 8

"We met with the Indians on the twentieth and on the twenty-first the treaty was signed."

The landmark treaty that would eventually cover roughly 841,487 square kilometres, including portions of northern Alberta, northwest Saskatchewan and the modern Northwest Territories and BC, was ostensibly negotiated between two sovereign nations in less than twenty-four hours on June 20 and 21, 1899, through a Cree-English interpreter whose linguistic skills were questionable. How could even the best translator explain in just one day, in his second language, complex concepts like extinguishment and allodial title to Nehiyawak who didn't speak English and had no Western education?

The Government of Canada offered the chiefs it had appointed one-time and ongoing benefits far greater than what the other Nehiyawak would receive, setting up a corrupt and inequitable system that persists to this day.

> And with a view to show the satisfaction of Her Majesty with the behaviour and good conduct of Her Indians, and in extinguishment of all their past claims, She hereby, through Her Commissioners, agrees to make each Chief a present of thirty-two dollars in cash, to each Headman twenty-two dollars, and to every other Indian of whatever age, of the families represented at the time and place of the payment, twelve dollars.

The arrival of the treaty commission was delayed by three weeks, supposedly because of weather. The commission arrived in late June, a crucial harvest time. Many Cree individuals and families had returned to the land and as a result were excluded. Although the commission said government representatives would be back to deal with this important flaw in the process, no subsequent effort was undertaken to contact those individuals or families to include them.

Treaty 8 was never properly ratified, even though the institution of ratification existed as early as the 1700s. Under a ratification process, the treaty commission would have had to take Treaty 8 before the Parliament of Canada for a vote, and this, only after the four government-appointed chiefs had enumerated and registered the people they represented, then conducted a vote that would have had to meet a certain threshold to indicate approval. The modern threshold for community approval of treaties with Canada is a double majority—51 per cent who vote in favour, with at least 50 per cent of the population voting. I have not found any evidence that Treaty 8 was ratified by either the Parliament of Canada or

the Cree people whose rights and title were supposedly extin-
guished by the document in question.

The excerpts above are from the report of the Treaty 8
commissioner to the minister of the interior and from the text of
Treaty 8, respectively.

Yekooche

I COULD BARELY KEEP up with elder Catherine Bird as she sped through the now dense, now clear-cut forest to get to Yekooche, a Dakelh village eighty kilometres north of Fort St. James, British Columbia. It was June 1990, and the local school district had been asked by Tl'azt'en First Nation to take over the community school in Yekooche from the Department of Indian and Northern Affairs the next fall.

Why was Catherine in such a rush? Was she testing me— curious to see if a Cree boy turned city slicker, now a rural school principal driving a new cherry-red Suzuki Sidekick, could keep up with her older crimson Dodge pickup? We hydroplaned over vast puddles, shimmied over uneven washboards and plowed through a layer of fresh gravel before slowing to cross the tiny wooden bridge that spanned a moat around the village. I didn't dare take time to admire the new leaves that shimmered on stands of alder trees filtering the spring sun. I had forgotten how fine dust clogs the sinuses.

What would these people think of me? Could they accept me as a fellow Indian, even though I was a mixed-blood Cree who had an expensive haircut and fancy clothes and who spoke eloquent English? Fitting in was critical, though I wasn't sure why. I thought about how Catherine had confronted me the day before on the steps of the school district offices in front of my new boss, Louise Burgart, the assistant superintendent.

"*Hadih*—so you're Cree, eh? They're our neh-bors and eh-nemy—stole our horses 'n womans." Looking stern, she paused, glanced from me to Louise, who was blonde and at least six inches taller than Catherine, then back at me again. Once Louise's cheeks had pinkened and my eyebrows had furrowed, Catherine let out a loud girlish laugh. "I jus' lie—good to have you here, T'airl." She stretched out her eagle-claw hand and clasped mine. Her hand was as strong as Mother's, though it wasn't a man hand like Mother's had been. No, I decided, Catherine wasn't testing me, she was just doing what she always did. She knew these back roads like the face of her eldest child.

Chaos. That was the only word to describe what was going on in the classroom I visited in the dilapidated schoolhouse the next morning right after recess. I was the only visitor to venture in—the Indian Affairs director, Juanita Tupper, and my boss, Louise, waited outside. A warped forty-five vinyl record of a Beatles song played on the small school-issue turntable, the melody wafting in and out. *I -ee wah na ... hol...yor... ha-a-a... wah na...hol... your ha-a...*

Then a witch. That was honestly what I thought I saw. A woman with long, matted grey hair, a wrinkled face, missing teeth and chipped and gritty fingernails was perched behind her desk fidgeting with some papers. Instant tears, which I blinked back. About fifteen kids with thick black hair were scattered around in one cluster on the floor by a cluttered bookshelf, a few cutting something out at a table covered with junk. Others were at their desks doing arithmetic worksheets. Torn textbooks and tattered paperbacks lay on the floor and countertop as if they had been flung there. Many curious glances in my direction, but everyone was too shy to say anything. Did they see me as I hoped, as another Indian who wanted to help them get out of the rut of poverty, dysfunction and sorrow, or were they even aware of their situation? Did they care in the slightest way who I was? Through the bank of windows I could see large crows flitting between tall spruce trees and alders, cawing over each other impatiently and making guttural clicking noises. I thought of home—Spurfield, and the dozens of cousins I grew up with in Smith, Alberta. We all had thick black hair like that. Classes had been organized, clean and strict at our school, but the crows outside were identical.

That afternoon, I strolled to the cemetery at the edge of town and paused beside the white picket fence around one grave. I looked toward Shass Mountain and began to pray—not to Jesus or to God, but to the ancestors of this place. I asked them to accept me, to protect me and guide me to do the best I could to help their descendants.

At two in the morning in a cabin along the shores of Stuart Lake, I woke with a sucking hollowness in my chest. Was I really going to do this—move north on my own, leaving my teaching job and friends in Vancouver? More importantly, was I going to leave Milan? When the emptiness didn't recede, I lay in the dark, thinking. I pictured my classroom at Trafalgar Elementary, on the west side of Vancouver, and wondered how my students would have reacted had they seen Yekooche, the school building and the students—the beauty, the starkness, the unkemptness and the abject poverty. I thought about the contrast between my well-equipped and neatly organized classroom, tastefully decorated with student art, and what I had seen at the Portage School. I would have to get rid of everything but the furniture and start anew. What would we do for phys. ed.? There was no gym or even a playground. I would have to recruit an entirely new team of teachers, and that wouldn't be easy. The next day I would need to start ordering books and poring over résumés.

I tried to lull myself to sleep by picturing Milan's bulky hands and his kind, loving gaze. Milan had purchased a trendy condominium in Kitsilano, where we had settled into a comfortable life with a circle of caring friends, the type of friends I could only have dreamed of having in northern Alberta or in Calgary—teachers, a school principal, a physiotherapist, a Guatemalan friend and one who was Rotuman. Weekly dinner parties. Weekend mornings at Granville Island Public Market enjoying coffee and croissants while we listened to buskers were followed by hours of me singing my favourite tunes and accompanying myself on piano or guitar at home. Surely Milan would stick with me through the transition to working and living in Yekooche. He had been so supportive in my university years, through my five years of teaching and through my sorrow when first my sister Debbie died, and then Mother.

Why was I making this drastic change in my life? Was I trying to rebuild my connection with Cree culture after losing my only bridge to it—Mother? Was I trying to get back to my roots, or was it simply more escapism, a distraction to avoid my predicament—a collapsed and diminishing family, sexual confusion, an uncertain future, a constant fear of falling into a downward spiral and losing everything?

The next day over a lunch of Chinese Combo C at the King's Inn, the frumpy but energetic Indigenous education resource teacher for the school district asked me in her peculiar British accent, "Do you have any idee-*er whot* you are getting into? Just last week there was a crisis in the communit-*ih.* A young man they call John-John wandered through town shooting his hunting rifle into the air—nobody could stop him. And many people in Fort St. James will show you the bullet holes in their vehicles from when they worked in the bush near Yekooche. Not only that, my friend, you have an im-*po*-ssible job. Too much inbreeding—everyone's last name is the same. Didn't they tell you? Who would *ever* want to work *there*?"

"I'm not worried or afraid. I come from a community like that," I said stoically. What I was really thinking was that I had prayed to the ancestors at Yekooche—they would protect and guide me. "Oh, and Toni, with respect to inbreeding, I read somewhere that this has actually been a problem with the British royal family. Is that true?"

❖

"There's a rock in t'err." Tilly peered up at me with bloodshot eyes that were partially concealed by frayed black hair. We were standing on the porch of my temporary home, a large trailer beside the school, eating peaches from the bushel I had bought as I passed through Kamloops. It was August by now, and I had been in Yekooche for a month.

"It's not a rock, it's the pit. This is a peach, Tilly."

"A pit! What fer?"

"The seed, Tilly, to grow a new peach tree."

"*Hadih*—none of d'em kinda trees aroun' here!"

How I handled Tilly's visit would send a message to all the other kids, or at least that was my intent. If you wanted to meet the new *prin*-ci-*pl*, you'd have to sit outside with him on the porch steps to visit. It may have seemed strange that I didn't invite them in, especially to the teenagers used to visiting the former principal in his trailer. In my head I was very clear about why, though I couldn't bring myself to tell them. I thought about my farewell lunch in Vancouver with my friend Linda.

"So, you're going north to sexually abuse children, Darrel? Is that why you became a principal in a remote Native community?" Linda raised her right hand, palm up, and looked me in the eye. She was a sign language interpreter at Trafalgar Elementary and a lesbian activist who had taken training in sexual abuse prevention and now considered herself an expert.

I was dumbfounded. "Are you out of your mind, Linda?"

"Victims often become perpetrators—I had to ask."

Linda's line of questioning was like a forging fire. My determination to protect the children in my new school grew steelier than ever. In fact, I became obsessed with it. Everyone in Yekooche probably thought I was a cold fish, and luckily I only had to enforce my policy once when the high school teacher, Randy Wallace, told me he had let a couple of boys sleep over in his trailer one night to bond. I ordered him to never repeat that.

❖

Marlene and Robert McCracken, the whole-language gurus, were giving a week-long workshop in Monterey, California, late that summer, and I knew I had to go. Whole language was at the avant-garde of English language instruction methodology and its advocates were convincingly charismatic.

"Well, there *is* money in your budget for professional development, Darrel, and this would be amazing. We can't cover travel costs, but the rest would be fine," my boss, Louise, bubbled.

"I'd like to take the whole team, Louise: Catherine, Leona, Debbie and myself."

"Hmmm. I'm not sure what the perception of that will be in the district—professional development in California. Tell your team to keep it quiet when you guys start up in September."

Catherine Bird was no less confident driving through the California redwood forest than she had been flying through the boreal forest of northern BC. She shifted gears in my cherry Sidekick as if she were driving an eighteen-wheeler. We had got to know each other quickly, proving that the saying "Sudden acquaintance brings repentance" is not always true. The more we talked, the more we bonded, and we agreed—we were on a mission. In

Yekooche that fall, we would set up the best literacy and Carrier language programs anyone had ever seen.

"You havta write your own stories down, T'airl. They will help others," Catherine insisted one evening as the four of us sat in a trendy beachfront restaurant chatting after a long day. I had been telling them the story of my prospective singing debut at the age of nine—how it was cancelled because Mother had left home and I couldn't find anyone else to give me a haircut. Mrs. Earl, my Grade Four homeroom and choir teacher, had given me an ultimatum—get a haircut or no solo. "Old Bonebags" was sung by the choir instead, while I stood at the back blubbering.

Catherine told us about raising her eleven kids as a single mother after her husband passed away, how she had become a hunter and a skilled outdoorswoman to provide for her family. Later in life, her mastery of Dakelh, the local dialect, had helped her to get training as a teacher.

❖

"I'm Darrel; this is Debbie, Leona, Mrs. Bird and Mr. Wallace," I announced at the assembly on the first day of school. "You already know Art and Sally, the teaching assistants." In Monterey we had discussed how we wanted to be addressed by the students, and I was respecting the teachers' wishes to use either their first names or their proper titles. Instead of being crammed into a stuffy gymnasium, we were gathered on the shore of Babine Lake. Some men and older teenaged boys from the community had just pulled in their large nets, which were overflowing with frisky sockeye salmon. Catherine, Art, Sally and I had finished cooking and serving pancakes, bacon, eggs and hash browns to the students, parents and grandparents who had come to the week-long fish camp we'd set up to inaugurate the school year. After people had finished eating, Catherine made an announcement in Dakelh and we split into groups for morning activities. We knew we had to keep our opening remarks brief—the men and elders needed to get started on preparing and preserving the fish.

Early that afternoon, after sampling a soup made with the heads, spines and roe of salmon, along with celery, potatoes and onions, I went over to the round smokehouse where the women elders sat on the ground cutting fish, sipping Labrador tea, talking and giggling. They were so graceful at cutting open the oily red fish and then butterflying each side once more to create four connected flaps that they threaded onto a long pole. They gave me a sharp knife and watched as I awkwardly sliced a salmon into four jagged flaps. They laughed at my clumsiness with the knife, but I felt like I belonged.

The next afternoon I went blackberry picking on the hillside. These definitely weren't the blackberries that grew on the coast. They resembled blueberries and tasted similar, but were on taller bushes. Some of the smaller kids joined me, and when we had almost filled one bucket, a stocky boy named Isaac sauntered over and muttered, "Prin-ci-pl—Monique, she wanna see you. That hers cabin at da bot'um o' da' hil."

"Okay, tell her I'll be right there."

I had met Monique when I first arrived. Her aged husband, Abel, reminded me of my great-grandfather Joseph Powder, my *mosom*—he didn't speak English and was a serious provider, always trapping, hunting and harvesting plants, ensuring the smoke-house out back of his tiny cabin near Spurfield, Alberta, was never empty. My mother, two siblings and I had lived there with Mosom until I was five. He chewed snuff and smoked a pipe briefly in the evening to relax. I wondered if Abel chanted and drummed in the early morning like Mosom had.

Monique was the matriarch of one of the two large Joseph families in the community. She had lots of children, and they in turn had children and in some cases grandchildren. So far I had met Art, who was in his fifties and worked at the school, and Henry, her next eldest. John-John was her youngest.

Monique was very much like my Auntie Helen and my Cucuum Philomene, with her wind-worn squarish face and prominent cheeks, except that she was heftier and much more direct than any of my aunties. It was her advice that had helped me set the school up for success, though I knew I couldn't follow everything she said literally. "No use startin' school first week o' Se'tember— we gotta fish 'n hunt ta get food for da' winter. We all go across't t'a Babine fer a week or two. An' Fridays—forget Fridays. E'ryone gotta go down ta town ta cash cheques, go shoppin' 'n play bingo. 'N t'em teen-agers—t'ey can't sit in school for hours 'n hours lis'nin' and writin' stuff down—gotta be out 'n about doin' stuff. Learnin' thin's t'ey can use right now. And t'at Isaac, sometimes he be real stubborn. You jus' grab that son-o-bitch by the hair an' tell 'em he has ta listen. Tell 'em Monique gif' you permission."

Louise had supported me completely when I met with Mike Fitzpatrick, the district superintendent, to tell him that I wanted to start the school year with a week-long fish camp at Babine Lake, and that I wanted the school to operate on a four-day week.

Now I stood in Monique's doorway, smiling, wondering what she would say this time.

"*Hadih*, principl'. See y're pickin' d'em berries. T'ose are mine—t'is is my territor-ih."

I could feel her power. I was surprised she was confronting me, and I hoped she wouldn't notice that I was shaking slightly. I moved closer and extended my hand.

"*Tansi*, Monique. Nice to see you again. Yes, I know. These are your berries and this is your territory. I was picking them for *you*—in this bucket I swiped from your porch," I answered with a nervous chuckle.

"*Hadih. Mussi cho.* Where you from anaways?"

"I'm Cree from around Lesser Slave Lake. Grew up there mostly, but went to high school in Calgary and lived in Vancouver too."

"So, you're Dakelh? *Hadih*, we got a Dakelh prin-ci-pl."

"Close enough," I said with a chuckle.

From then on, Monique was one of my staunchest allies.

That night, sitting around the campfire with the school staff and a few parents, I prompted a round of laughter as I told a story about the kids calling out to Catherine and Randy during the day's activities. *Mista' Bird, Mista' Bird—help me with my kite. Missus Wallus—Missus Wallus—come see how we set net to catch salmon.* No matter how many times Catherine and Randy corrected the children, they were stuck with Mr. Bird and Mrs. Wallace. I felt content, welcome and respected, but I missed Milan and could hardly wait to get to Fort St. James to call him from a pay phone. I hadn't yet told anyone about him and the significant role he played in my life.

❖

Normal classes were set to begin the second week of September for everyone except the teenagers, who were at an outdoor camp to learn orienteering, survival skills, canoeing and Dakelh language. In the weeks to come, the older students would have workshops instead of regular classes—hairstyling, baking, basic cooking, drum making, hide tanning and other skills to build their self-confidence and give them a positive experience at school. The plan was that we would ease them into a more structured academic program in November.

By 9:15 on the Monday of the second week, only a handful of the seventy or so students we had registered had showed up. So at 8:00 a.m. on the Tuesday, standing on the steps of the school, I played "Reveille" on my high school trumpet. I was on my third round of "ta-*ta*-tadada ta-*ta*-tadada" when Art pulled up in his pickup truck and began honking his horn in rhythm with my playing.

"*Hadih*. Ever craz-ih, prin-ci-pl," Art called out as he studied me, his head cocked to one side.

Everyone thought I was joking when I announced later that day that the whole school—students, teachers, assistants, the secretary and I—would begin a mandatory fitness program: every day, twenty minutes before morning recess, we would go for a run or a walk. Sally and Art were lined up to serve hot soup and bannock to each person as they returned, a role the teenagers would take over once back from camp.

The next day, around 11:00 a.m., we got a surprise visit from the district superintendent. Mike spent a half-hour in the school, observing and scribbling notes. "You have your staff dressed nicely—so professional," he said in a singsong voice as he stepped out onto the porch and offered me his hand. Mike's timing couldn't have been better. Art and a few other men had just driven up to the school with truckloads of smoked and dried salmon, jars of bear grease, a pile of bear meat, tanned hides and a quartered moose to show the kids what we had accomplished during our week at the fish camp.

❖

By the end of September, though, I was discouraged. Randy was having problems with the teenagers' behaviour. I'd learned that Isaac and a couple of other teens were sniffing gas. Leona and I had discovered that the literacy challenges with the intermediate class were even greater than we had thought. A few of the primary children had emotional problems we couldn't address. Our book order was late. The telephone system we had hoped the band would install would cost five thousand dollars and there was no budget for it, so we were stuck with the expensive and unreliable radio phone.

The previous Friday, when the band manager invited me to Taché, the larger community across the lake, for a meeting, I had hoped for good news. Instead, he gave me an ominous warning about getting involved in the politics of the community. The Yekooche elders were upset about how they were being treated by the larger community, the Tl'azt'en Nation, who administered their affairs, and they wanted to separate. The band manager was afraid that I would help them with this. Our conversation, or rather his monologue, went like this:

"You're not gonna help 'em with this, mister. Last princip!' tried. Keep your nose out of it. Oh, 'n the construction of the new school's been delayed—won't turn the sod before next spring, but yer house should be ready by middle of October. You won' havta stay in that camper much longer. Nice o' ya ta give the trailers ta yer teachers."

I wasn't aware, but the *Dunne Za*—the top hereditary leader who was also the elected chief—was about to enter a turbulent time in his leadership. In fact, he had just bought a white elephant with a large settlement the community received—a cement plant, complete with trucks, that never returned to operation mode.

The moment I got back to Yekooche from Taché, I knew I had to return to the cemetery to plead with the ancestors. It was all getting to be too much. I set out from the school to walk the kilometre or so along the main road, which ran parallel to the creek. The fresh air and idyllic country setting calmed me. As I walked, I reminded myself why I was here. For years I had longed to be surrounded by empathetic brown faces, as I had been in my childhood. I'd missed hearing Cree spoken fluently, its comforting musicality. The language spoken here was Dakelh, a Dene language, but that didn't matter—it was beautiful too. I wanted to harvest and feast on traditional foods, re-establish my oneness with nature. Along with all of this, I hoped to reduce the misery and suffering in this forsaken and exploited community. If I could make a difference in the lives of even a few Yekooche children or adults by walking alongside them for a while, my purpose would be accomplished and I could move on.

Henry Joseph spotted me through the picture window of his house, a two-room shack where he and his wife, Lorna, lived with their seven kids, and came out to join me. I told him my woes.

"Why ya don't go ta the church ta pray? Agnes, she has the keys."

"I pray differently, Henry. I don't believe in all that stuff anymore—Jesus dying for my sins, heaven and hell."

"I don' wanna believe it too, but it's all we know. Four generations, maybe five all been ta residential school at Lejac. I don't wanna believe in hell, but I can't talk about that—can' even let myself think about it. I get scared."

I thought about the prayers the elders gave at the opening of events and meetings. Even though the prayers were in Dakelh, they always began with the sign of the cross, and Jesus's name would be sprinkled throughout.

As we strolled, Henry described the uniform he had had to wear for the marching band he played in as a boy at the Lejac residential school. He described the animosity between boys from different regions and how that continued to this day, then spoke more about the deep fear of ending up in purgatory or hell the priests and nuns had instilled in him and others.

Henry avoided the bull moose in the room, and so did I—sexual and physical abuse by the priests and nuns—but I didn't know how he could have escaped it. We strolled along the dirt road side by side in silence for another ten minutes or so, my heart pounding with excitement. This was the type of connection and acceptance I had come here for.

That Friday night, around ten o'clock, I bumped into Henry outside the five-and-dime store in downtown Fort St. James, not far from the notorious bar everyone called the Zoo. He saw me as

I was coming out with a can of Dr Pepper and a bag of Old Dutch chips, walked over and flashed his disarming smile. Even with a few missing teeth and wrinkles from stress and drinking, he was still handsome.

"*Hadih*, T'airl. *T'su in' t'oh*," he said as he moved in close. His breath had that all-too-familiar sour fermented malt smell, and his eyes were glazed and bloodshot.

"*T'su 'us t'oh*," I answered.

"*Hadih*. You learn fast. Goot ta see ya. Hey—kin ya lend me ten bucks, jus' need ten bucks—pay ya back nex' week."

"Henry, you already bin drinkin', man. Can't give you money to go drink it up."

He paused for a second. Then his smile vanished, and his eyes became glassy marbles. His gaze burned into mine as he body-slammed me against the coarse stucco wall of the store, and my pop and chips went flying. His sturdy hands were suddenly around my throat, squeezing.

"I could fuckin' kill you, man—right here, right now." Droplets of his saliva sprayed my face. I blinked and stiffened. I peered directly into his eyes and summoned as much ch'i as I could.

"I know, Henry." I strained, then paused a second to peer into his glassy eyes. He was way stronger than me, but I raised my hands onto his shoulders to try to calm him—also to push back hard if it came to that.

"Yes, you could kill me—for sure, Henry. But you won't. I'm your friend. Your brother."

❖

"You don't look Native": it was a common reaction when I told white locals in Fort St. James, Vanderhoof or Prince George that I was Cree. I knew what they were really saying—you don't appear down-and-out like the Indians around here. At the fall barbecue the education director of Tl'azt'en First Nation threw for the teachers from Yekooche and Taché, a few people told me the same thing. One teacher, Alex, was adamant about it. "Filipino or Chinese, maybe," he said.

"Alex, Darrel is Cree from Alberta," the director's wife scolded him. "The school district checked his background and references before hiring him."

Unfazed, Alex grabbed his guitar and pulled his chair closer. He slid one of his meaty, jean-clad thighs between mine, and before I could pull my chair back or sit up straight he started strumming his guitar while plucking a strong bass line on the back beat. His voice was a tenor like mine but more natural, no vibrato and more rasp. He sang a song I'd never heard before, about becoming lovers and marrying fortunes together, regarding me intensely the whole time. I felt myself flush.

I was sure everyone was staring at the two of us, but Alex didn't seem to care. Thankfully the rest of the lyrics were abstract— the ending talked about looking for America. Generous applause. Alex nodded at the group, smiled and handed me the guitar.

"I hear you play."

"Yeah, but not nearly as well as you."

"C'mon. Show us what you've got."

I started Travis picking, then launched into "Beautiful" by Gordon Lightfoot. Ugh, why had I chosen the sappiest love song I knew? Would people think my song was in response to Alex's barely veiled invitation?

Alex invited me back to his house after the barbecue. I was worried what people would think—just what I needed, to start the school year off with rumours—but I went anyway. I was astonished to find a full PA system in his living room. He set me up with a mic, connected his guitar and passed it to me. He asked me to perform "Beautiful" again. "Put your heart into it," he said.

This time I was more intent in my performance, holding his powerful gaze as best I could.

"You'll have to come back next weekend, my man. My girl-friend will be here, but she'll be busy with her two kids."

As I drove through Fort St. James on my way back to Yekooche, I stopped to call Milan. When I heard him say my name with glee, I felt guilty. He must have sensed something different in my voice as I told him about the evening. "D.J., you can't sit on two chairs," he said. "You'll have to choose."

"What do you mean, Milan? Everything's fine. I'll see you in a couple of weeks in Vancouver, okay?"

❖

"Jump, Darrel—now! Jump up and down fast. Wave your arms and yell!"

"Alex. What the hell?"

"Whoooo whoooo, it's us. We're from Taché! *Aaeeeiiiieeyyy!*" Alex screamed.

"Whooooooooo hooooooooo! Aaiiiiiiiiyyy." Bewildered, I echoed his cry.

"Now hit the ground," he yelled as he threw himself down and pulled his springer spaniel, Ché, in close.

I dropped to the ground as ordered. "What's going on?"

"Listen."

A boat motor in the distance, faint but getting louder.

"Hunters. With powerful rifles and scopes. They had us in their sights, I could feel it."

Alex slung his arm over my shoulder as we walked back to his house. I loved the affection I got from him, but secretly hoped nobody saw us like that. When we got home, we planned to roast the goose one of the teen boys from Yekooche had given me.

After we'd eaten, Alex raved about the meal, how juicy and succulent. "Way better than domestic goose," he sighed with contentment. "We'll go bird hunting next weekend. Get some grouse, blue or spruce. Maybe duck. They're all delicious."

That night in his living room, Alex announced he wanted to do some improvisation, with him playing chord progressions and me inventing melodies. He laughed when my first attempt came out with "one, two, three, four, five six, seven, nine" as the lyrics.

"Are we composing kindergarten songs or what?"

I found a melody I liked and repeated it. I sang it to "la" for a while, and then to my surprise Cree words started to come out of my mouth, lyrics Mother had sung to a Hank Williams tune: "*Ki wîhkâc peyagun tapscotch niya.*" I hadn't heard her Cree version of "May You Never Be Alone" since before she'd left home when I was ten. I sang it over and over with Alex's accompaniment, tears streaming down my face.

After a few minutes, Alex stopped playing, came over and pulled me into a hug. "Come on—let's take a break." He sat down and patted the couch beside him.

I rested my head on his shoulder, tears still leaking out of my eyes. I loved the power of his aura, but I felt silly.

"That was beautiful. Don't ever hold back your emotions, my man. Let go when they come on strong like that. What was going through your mind?"

"Well, I saw my mother. She died last year of cancer. She used to sing that song late at night when she was drinking. She and Mosom, my great-grandfather, were here dancing around the room to our music."

"Here, let me blow out the candles. Get comfortable."

Alex eased me into a lying position, then he stretched out beside me, pulling me in so close I was breathing his exhalation. Shyly, I placed my arm over his chest. After a half-hour or so, I got bolder—I unbuttoned his shirt, slid my hand inside and kept it there.

I had a new glow as I drove back to Yekooche the next afternoon. Alex had accompanied me as far as Fort St. James, and we'd eaten Chinese food at King's Inn. There were lots of people from

Yekooche and Taché there having an early dinner. Did they sense the romantic connection between Alex and me? It didn't matter. All we'd done was share a lovely dinner and cuddle, and Alex's friendship and warmth had helped to mollify the longing I felt day and night to be with Milan and my close friends in Vancouver.

❖

My visit to Vancouver the next long weekend was surreal. I was excited to return to the city and have time at home with Milan. I'd brought a good-sized steelhead trout and moose tongue for him and our close friends, Ted and Yolande, John and Sheila, to sample.

On the Saturday morning Milan and I followed our weekend routine: we enjoyed a *caffe latte* and croissant at the Blue Parrot on Granville Island while reading the *Vancouver Sun*, then perused the market stands for tasty vegetables and fruit, stopping to listen to buskers between purchases. Later I went to the hairstylist who was skilled at shaping my wiry and wavy hair into a low-maintenance cut. Sporting my new hairdo I went downtown to window shop.

I used to love days like this, but it wasn't the same—something had shifted in me. I missed the serenity of Stuart Lake, the forest, wildlife and the disarming sincerity of the people of Yekooche. The urban anonymity I used to bask in now troubled me. I felt lost in the sea of indifference of the people milling about or hustling past me.

When I got back to our condo in Kitsilano I rushed to look at myself in the mirror. The hairstyle I had thought was *très chic* in the salon made me seem effeminate.

Milan had invited our friends over for dinner so I prepared the moose tongue as an appetizer the way I'd seen Mother do. I sliced it thinly against the grain and served it with rye wafers, baby dills and Dijon mustard. To my dismay, my friends wouldn't touch it.

❖

The drive from Fort St. James to Yekooche was bumpy and dusty but uneventful, with time for me to mull over my weekend visit to Vancouver—the Thanksgiving dinner Milan had organized. It was great to see my friends, but I wasn't sure where I belonged anymore. What if I fell into a chasm between two solitudes? The next weekend I was planning a trip to Taché to see Alex and my Turkish friend Umit, who taught high school there. I'd brought back some Wild Turkey bourbon and a couple of packs of Gitanes cigarettes from the city for Umit and me to enjoy. A bundle of foreign magazines, too.

My thoughts were interrupted by a black bear that dashed from the ditch into the forest. A couple of logging trucks zoomed by in the opposite direction, their loads swaying in the wind. I pulled into a turnoff for a pee.

A kilometre or so along the road to Yekooche, I noticed a couple of pickup trucks parked along the curb. Four men huddled near the edge of the forest, absorbed in studying something on the ground. I stopped and headed in their direction for a better look. It was big Alan, Art with his son Chris, and Dean.

"*Hadih*, principl', come over here," Alan yelled.

"All right! Let's see what a Cree boy from the city can do," Dean called out.

When I got closer I saw they were kneeling alongside a huge bull moose, its antlers rotated to one side.

"You wanna clean 'im principl'? Ya havta be real careful. If you do it wrong, you can spoil the meat."

Panic flooded my body, then a thrill. You can do this, Darrel, I thought. You've always wanted to clean a moose. You've cleaned rabbits—dissected rats and a fetal pig. And you've watched people butcher and clean moose and deer many times.

Alan fetched a large blue tarp from his truck, and the men slid it under the moose, rotating the carcass until the animal was on its back with its glossy eyes staring right at me, each pupil a sideways oval.

The moment wasn't lost on me. The men weren't sloughing off their work, they were honouring me. Intense emotions welled up but I held them back. Be calm, Darrel. Focus. Don't blow this.

I inserted the large hunting knife Alan handed me just below the sternum and pushed the blade toward the animal's anus, cautious not to perforate the bowel. Then I came back to the starting point, reinserted the metal blade and slit the skin in the other direction. When I pulled the skin flaps apart, a pungent vapour escaped, overwhelming me. My glasses steamed up. I'd have to feel my way around. I held my breath. I slid one hand inside the throat along the windpipe, then grasped its distal end. I inserted the knife carefully again—no bowels to perforate up there, but I didn't want to cut myself. My sleeves were completely soaked with blood by now and oh my god, the odour. I thought I was going to faint.

It took all my strength to cut the esophagus and the windpipe. I pulled them away from the spine, slicing the connective tissue with my other hand.

Next I had to cut the intestinal and urinary tracts. I'd watched a pathologist pull the same mass of organs out of a human cadaver in one fell swoop on my second day of work as an orderly at Vancouver General Hospital, and I knew it would impress the men if I could do the same. I cut the tissue up and down the body cavity, then pulled gently but steadily, using my own body weight for leverage.

Still on their knees, the Yekooche men shuffled in closer. I felt their body warmth as I pulled the entrails out in one bunch. The four of them swung into action. One went for the liver, another for the heart and yet another for the lungs. The bible. They knew the elders' tastes and would deliver the organ meats accordingly.

"T'airl, I'll stop by tomorrow with the head and the tenderloin—you can have the tongue and nose, too, but I want the antlers," Alan said, sounding apologetic.

As I glanced at my hands, covered in drying and clotted blood, a shiver rolled through me. For a second, I was sure I'd seen Mother's hands in place of mine. As a boy I had loved watching her bulky hands skilfully slice and separate sinew from flesh. I felt a pang of joy. It intensified as I strode back to my vehicle to continue on to Yekooche.

Whiteout

OH, MY GOD! Right outside my window, men in white hoods are setting fire to crude wooden crosses. Why are they targeting me—because I'm Nehiyaw? Or do they think I'm gay? They're milling about in the clearing, in front of a stack of seasoned timber, their torches held high. How did they find me here in my rustic cabin, nestled on this hillside between the Trans-Canada Highway and the CNR tracks, metres above the lake?

Who should I call? I'm sure the RCMP won't believe me. They'll think I'm insane or hallucinating. Lord Jesus, more men are arriving! A steady procession—single file—some tall, others short—pointy hoods bobbing up and down as they march. More torches.

"*Sieg heil*—blood and soil," one man calls. A chorus of muffled, monotone voices echoes his cry: "*Sieg heil...* blood... so-yal... Blooood 'n soy-all."

Fuck, if they're not careful, they'll burn the whole place down, and the fire will spread into the forest. Is that what they want—to torch this shack, with me in it? Oh god, there's no one else around—no neighbours, no tourists. It's useless to call for help. How can I challenge them, or at least escape?

❖

Dissonant squawks and honks from the Canada geese launching overhead awoke me. What time? Didn't matter. My mind was in spirals, my temples throbbing. I jumped up, threw on a shirt and a pair of pants, spit on my hands and patted down my hair, then stumbled outside and across the dew-speckled grass. Songbirds rejoicing. An acrid odour that could only be a skunk. I hoped it wasn't nearby.

Damn, the seats in my Suzuki Sidekick were wet. I'd left the rooftop open overnight—again. Milan would've scolded me. Through the rectangular opening, a falling sky: leaves of alder and trembling aspen danced worriedly against a Crayola-blue background. I paused for a moment and took a deep breath. The purr of the engine beckoned me to shift into first gear, ease up on the clutch and release the brake to roll up the narrow country lane to the safety of the highway. Grateful for being alive, I tried to calm myself.

I'd just settled in Salmon Arm after a move from Yekooche and it was idyllic—the lake, the surrounding hills and the wildlife. I missed Art and Sally, Dean and the students, but I could still visit them, and in Salmon Arm I would meet new people. The winter was less extreme, no hazardous logging road to drive a few times a week, less violence. This was the rationale I had come up with for the dramatic decision to leave Yekooche after only one year. I hadn't taken time to consider what was really going on in my mind and heart. Had I been motivated by fear? My life *had* been threatened twice in the short time I was there and I'd already begun to be an activist for the community even though I'd been warned not to. And my relationship with the people in Yekooche seemed too good to be true. Although we'd taken a "don't ask, don't tell" approach to my personal life, I knew I couldn't suppress the reality of who I was forever. Sooner or later it would come out that I was in a relationship with a man in Vancouver and was getting emotionally involved with another—Alex. Once word got around, life would have become untenable. Dangerous.

In my new job, I'd get to travel all over BC to work with many First Nations, urban and rural, developing college-level education programs and curricula. I was much closer to Vancouver—to Milan and my circle of friends—but as I arrived at the college, the KKK nightmare still weighed heavily.

As we stood by the coffee machine, swilling our first cup, I described my nightmare to Emil Auger, the tall young Nehiyaw man who had been the director of the provincial Native Adult Education Resource Centre—NAERC—before I was recruited to take over as its head. Emil had left in a cloud of gossip and scandal and was now a contractor for the centre. I wanted to get his views on the dream: was there some profound meaning in it, perhaps a warning?

A minute into my story, Ethan Swayer, the centre's founder, raised his eyebrows and offered me a crooked smile. Ethan and Emil exchanged curious glances. Did they think I was crazy, or did they know something they didn't want to reveal to me, a relative stranger? Confused and frustrated, I headed back to my office to delve into the pile of reading on my desk. I was determined to read every resource that NAERC had produced and to at least skim all the books we sold through our clearing house.

Shivers and a rush of tears surprised me when I came to the poem "I Am Not Your Princess" in a collection by a poet named Chrystos. Her bio said she was a self-educated two-spirit Menominee writer and activist. I'd never read anything so raw, or anything I related to on a gut level like that. Her poem was about being the sandpaper between two cultures. Instantly, I grasped that this was the position I was now in, and had also been in at Yekooche working for the local school district as principal. Maybe I could smooth the rough edges, the areas of friction between Indigenous and white culture, but at what cost? Sandpaper, once used, is left torn and ragged. Is that what I was in for?

As I read Chrystos's sombre recipe for making fry bread, I thought of Mother and of Catherine Bird, their enduring, wiry hands gently kneading the dough to produce a tender and delicious result. Was it the flavour of the bannock that I cherished, or was it the love and psychic energy Mother and Catherine put into their baking as they worked it? Not only *their* energy, but that of the line of strong Nehiyaw and Dakelh women they descended from, the essence of their double helices magically incorporated into the bannock.

I still had a dream about Mother at least once a week, even though she had been gone for three years. The dreams flummoxed me. In some, Mother had become a sort of zombie, her cadaver mobile and conversational. Clad in the outfit she was buried in, she cut a benign but horrific figure. In other dreams she was simply dead, her corpse as unsightly as the many I had handled as an orderly at the Rockyview General Hospital in Calgary and the Vancouver General Hospital, the same sour odour—nothing unique, other than it was Mother.

Instead of letting the dreams depress me, I was grateful for them. I understood that mourning Mother's loss would take time. Years later, an amazing Anishnabe woman, Kathy Absolon, would tell me that when deceased family members appear in dreams, they want to be feasted—honoured in ceremony with morsels of their favourite food.

❖

I wandered down to Sxstélenemx—Shuswap Lake—each day that summer after work with a towel and a blanket and swam back and forth, following the shoreline for safety, taking in the surrounding hills as I rolled my body from side to side in the front crawl. The water was refreshing—sweet to the taste—neutral to the eyes. This was my new form of exercise, along with an occasional visit to the gym.

At times, I was sure I sensed the presence of the legendary monster of the lake. On those days, I would dry off jittery and unsettled. Other days, swimming became a meditation: I turned myself over to the spirit of Sxstélenemx, letting her soothe and heal me. An electric charge would flash through me afterwards—ecstasy.

Ethan Swayer was a swimmer too, though much more proficient than I was. The first time I saw him emerge from the rec centre pool in his red Speedo, I was at once envious and embarrassed. He was a few years older than me, but very fit. His chest was muscular, as were his legs. My legs were muscular too, but my belly and chest were flabby.

Ethan liked to linger and chat poolside. His affable attitude was appealing, but he was white, tall and smart and he held power over me. Although I didn't know it at the time of my hiring, I had been brought on to be the passive brown face required for NAERC to maintain credibility with the government and First Nations. On paper, I was Ethan's boss, but he had recruited me and surely he could get rid of me easily too.

❖

"She has really romanticized bannock. It was Scottish flatbread introduced to Natives in North America at contact," Ross, a friend of Ethan's I'd recently hired as a program manager, scolded after I showed him Chrystos's poem and told him how it moved me. "I don't know what kind of starchy foods they had before that."

The information was correct, but his tone and the way he made his point bothered me. My ancestors had lived long and healthy lives, becoming octogenarians and beyond. Obviously they had had a complete diet. And if Ross really wanted to know what starchy food the Menominee and other tribes ate, he could have asked Mary Thomas, a revered Secwepemc elder who worked with us occasionally. Mary still harvested and prepared a panoply of traditional foods, including avalanche lily and tree lichen. The squares she made from grandfather's beard lichen were as tasty as any bread I'd ever eaten, and she said it had been a staple for the Secwepemc since time immemorial.

Another of Ross's rebukes hit me much harder. One morning as I walked past his desk to get a book from the storage room he called out, "Darrel, I have to say, just by looking at you I can tell you that you are not Cree. With a name like McLeod, you are Metis at best."

"Well, I am very proud of the Metis heritage on my father's side," I said. Locking my gaze with his, I continued, "It is a strong and fine line of true Metis blood, but Mother always referred to herself and to us as Nehiyaw, and my grandfather was a Cardinal. My grandfather, Mosom Jérémie, only spoke Cree, and our society is matrilineal. My great-grandfather was a Cree warrior on the plains. What's your heritage, Ross? Do you know?"

My response had been robust and rapid, but my self-confidence took a hit. I couldn't let the conversation end there. Mother's words—"You're Nehiyaw; always remember that and be proud"—rolled through my mind like a broken record. Early one morning I strode into Ross's office unannounced. He was at his desk, reading. I sat down across from him and without any niceties launched in.

"Listen, Ross. I know who I am, and I know the history of my people. My ancestors were starved into submission through the government-sponsored slaughter of the buffalo, forced to sign treaties and to move onto reserve lands. In my family's case it was even worse: the Indian commissioners negotiated Treaty 8 in the absence of the majority of my relations, without any community ratification process, saying they would be back. When they established the Indian register years later, many of my family members were left out—they still lived in family groupings in the bush."

My inner dragon was ignited. I was sick of being sandpaper.

"At the time Treaty 8 was negotiated, the federal government had stopped allocating reserves and instead granted parcels of land to individual families. Our family didn't get either, and we spiralled into poverty. So let me tell you, my friend, it hurts me tremendously to hear you question my identity. In the Northwest Territories, where you're from, the McLeods identify as Metis, but across the country there are also McLeods who are treaty and registered Indians. Please do your research before you challenge someone on something so fundamental as their identity. I know who I am—do you know who you are? Who are your ancestors, and what role did they play in the colonization of Canada, do you think?"

❖

I continued my reading, working my way through the books NAERC distributed. After a few pages of Beatrice Culleton Mosionier's novel *In Search of April Raintree*, I knew I needed to have a box of tissues nearby each time I opened it. It was the first time I had seen certain aspects of my own reality depicted in print. I hadn't been violently raped like the protagonist in the book, but my near-daily sexual abuse by Rory, a brother-in-law who was fourteen years my senior, was very damaging. As time passed I was coming to realize just how harmful it had been. And I had a sibling who had committed suicide—my oldest sister, Debbie, who had married Rory when she was just fifteen. April Raintree had two suicidal siblings. Not knowing this would soon be true for me, too, I couldn't imagine anyone coping with that level of loss.

Alone in the NAERC conference room one Sunday afternoon, I watched the documentary *Richard Cardinal: Cry from a Diary of a Métis Child*, directed by Alanis Obomsawin. It was about a young man who had a terrible life of physical and mental abuse in multiple foster homes throughout his childhood, until he finally committed suicide at age seventeen. I was astonished to discover that other Indigenous kids had actually had it worse—way worse—than my siblings and I had. After my sorrow subsided, the dragon inside of me began to rage. I knew I needed help to understand what was happening to me and to control my anger. The psychologist I sought out in Salmon Arm turned out to be amazing. "You have an incredible drive to be healthy," he told me at the end of our first meeting, "a strong will to live a vibrant life." I'd never thought of myself that way, but it was true. I continued to see him for a few months, and he referred me to a psychiatrist in Kelowna who specialized in helping male survivors of sexual abuse. I kept that a secret, though, even from Milan, who came to visit for long weekends whenever he could. When I bought my first house in downtown Salmon Arm, he stayed for two weeks to paint some of the rooms and help me get settled.

❖

Many weekends I went to visit Alex at the place he was renting just outside of Prince George, making the six-and-a-half-hour drive in just five. Alex had lots of time to practise the guitar and learn new songs since he had left his teaching job in Taché and was doing part-time freelance work. We refined the songs we had worked on together, like "More Than Words" by Extreme and a "All I Have to Do Is Dream" by the Everly Brothers, but Alex had learned more raucous songs like "Blaze of Glory" by Jon Bon Jovi and "Pour Some Sugar on Me" by Def Leppard, and although I belted out high-pitched harmonies above his vocals I did it *à contre-coeur* and squirmed in my chair as we sang. We spent a lot of time hugging and holding each other, and our emotional bond continued to deepen. There was no sex, but Alex fanned the flames of my ardour by saying things like, "You're handsome—a Native Clark Kent. If you were a woman, I'd make love to you right here and now."

One weekend I arrived late on Friday night, and by ten o'clock Saturday morning, Alex and I were canoeing down a small river that traversed boggy brush thoroughly infested with mosquitos and blackflies. The sky overhead, arctic blue, was hypnotic. I was perched on the front bench of the canoe, and Alex was at the back—the position of control. His spaniel, Ché, was huddled between us, tongue lolling, his stub of a tail wagging. We bounced along in turbulent water. Giggles, gleeful shouts. Yelps. I imagined I looked like a proud young Nehiyaw paddling at the front of the canoe, and I wished my family could see me like that. Even more, I wished they could join me.

After fifteen minutes of ecstasy, we navigated a blind curve only to face a barricade of fallen trees—sweepers—directly in front of us. Immediately past these was a solid wall of fallen logs, skinned branches protruding in every direction. The current propelled us toward the logjam with no time to apply the only brakes available to a canoeist—a brace or a backpaddle. Within seconds, our pointed bow had slammed against the largest log in the pile, and things began to unfold in slow motion.

Alex jolted to his feet and flashed past me to the bow as he hollered, "C'mon, c'mon. We gotta jump. Jump, jump, jump." He leapt onto the sturdiest log, pivoted quickly and jerked me beside him just as the canoe glided under the logjam.

"Good stuff. You did it, my man. Strong legs."

Our relief was short-lived. "What the hell are we supposed to do now?" Alex grumbled. "We're at least fifteen kilometres from the christly road in this dense goddamn brush. What the fuck are we supposed to do now? Wait, where's Ché? I lost my fucking dog. Wait a minute. The canoe is there—jammed under the logs—maybe Ché is still in it. C'mere. We have to rock this canoe and see if we can get it through. Hurry!"

I joined Alex, who was now knee-deep in the gushing water, with his butt pressed firmly against the logjam, pushing down on the gunwales with his feet. We rocked the canoe back and forth until we felt it glide under the logjam, then saw it emerge on the other side. Alex grabbed the rope attached to the bow and pulled on it with all his might. We managed to flip the canoe upside down. Just as we were pulling the boat out of the river, we heard a rustling in the bush. Ché emerged and ran toward us—his fur dripping wet, his tail stub wagging frenetically.

A month later, Alex and I were back canoeing on white-water—Onion Creek near Prince George. The frothy current and hyper-oxygenated air were exhilarating, but within a couple hundred metres, class three rapids became class four: raging flow, eddies and standing waves. We hadn't scouted the river, but we should have. When the bow of the canoe dipped dramatically downward, I leaned forward, slamming my oar across the gunwales.

"What the fuck are you doing, man? Paddle!" Alex shrieked.

"What am I s'posed ta paddle—air?" I answered as we flew over a six-foot chute—our *amerrissage* just beyond the whirlpool at the base of the falls. Ahead lay more rapids and reversing waves. Alex called out, "High brace. Forward paddle. PADDLE."

We directed the canoe ashore—leapt out, feet on packed sand—wobbly legs, breathless. Alex let out a resounding whoop, gave me a high-five. He threw his arms around my shoulders as he exclaimed, "We just came through class four water, man. My other canoeing buddy couldn'ta done that—you were awesome! I could fuck you."

That night, I didn't cuddle Alex. I lay on the mattress on his living room floor, alone, wondering if he had a death wish. Or was it me he was trying to kill?

A fall staff retreat at NAERC seemed like a good idea. Since the centre's Indigenous advisory board had collapsed over the preceding two years (too much conflict, Emil had explained one day over coffee), Ethan suggested we invite a Secwepemc woman, Rita Jack, to attend the retreat.

It all started out as a love-in. When Ethan introduced Rita as the first director of NAERC, I was impressed but puzzled—why hadn't he told me about her before? A mature Secwepemc woman with an M.Ed. on her CV and plenty of teaching and administrative experience, she was far more qualified for the job of director than either Emil or I were, and it was a plum job. So why had she left? The stress of doing a job that he wasn't adequately prepared for had affected Emil's life, and the same dynamic was increasingly robbing me of my peace of mind. There were demands from my boss, the college's dean, for accurate financial updates. Since the financial reports we got from the comptroller were always stale by months, we'd hired our own bookkeeper to keep a second set of books. A stack of curriculum projects didn't seem to be advancing. The college was demanding a large administrative overhead tied to our programming with local First Nations. The group assembled for the retreat had issues to discuss.

By the afternoon of the first day, the collegial ambience was giving way to growing animosity. Rita reminded us that in the initial proposal for NAERC, there was a commitment to hiring Indigenous staff in all key positions within three years. That deadline had passed two years earlier. At the moment, most of the consultants were white, and they were making good money, sixty thousand a year each or more. Ethan stammered and sighed, saying he needed to have somewhere else to land, also that it hadn't been easy finding qualified Indigenous educators or consultants, but Rita canvassed the Indigenous people present, and we agreed. Within a year the college should search for an Indigenous replacement for Ethan, or let Okanagan University College do it. We should also recruit more First Nations educators.

❖

My sister Gaylene called me at home a day after the retreat, and I was happy to hear a friendly voice without any hidden agenda or embedded political issues.

"Darrel, you need to sit down," she opened. "I have some amazing news, in two parts. First, I'm going to be the youngest *cucuum* ever, at age thirty-two. Jen's preggers—expecting a boy. And secondly... Listen now, you're gonna have to believe me on this. Everyone I've told so far's stopped me to say, 'Come on now, you're not gonna get me with that one.' Well, this is the plain truth, brother. We won the lottery. John and I. One point seventeen million dollars. But we love our lives and we think we'll keep working."

"*Mamaskatch*! I'll drive up to Edmonton this weekend." And I did. The first night we stayed home to celebrate, but the second night, Gaylene, Jen and I went out to play bingo at the Kingsway Mall.

Bingo. Things hadn't changed since I'd gone with Mother and Trina in Vancouver years earlier. In a haze of smoke, the crowd of women and a few gay men, mostly Indigenous, sat with their inky daubers, frantically flipping through a stack of twelve cards each to stain the numbers as they were called. Halfway through the first jackpot, Jen, who was seated across the table, suddenly slumped over and slid slowly from the bench toward the floor.

"Oh my god. My daughter's fainted—she's pregnant!"

A few women gasped. A couple more tittered and tsked. But nobody missed a beat with their daubing, and the caller kept the numbers coming. The smoke got thicker.

"Call 9-1-1," one woman yelled as she continued stamping her cards like a robot.

"For god's sake, what's wrong with you people?" Gaylene scolded as she and I pulled Jen into a sitting position. "You okay? You wanna keep playin' or go home?"

"I'll be okay," Jen whimpered.

I drove out of Edmonton in a light snow flurry at around 1:00 the next day, a Sunday. The snowfall was denser by the time I got to Hinton, but I had driven through much worse, so I continued. A couple of hours beyond Jasper, in the heart of the Rockies, there was a whiteout. I tapped the brake pedal, but it was too late: my Suzuki Sidekick spun like a car on the Tilt-a-Whirl ride at the fairground, except that my vehicle twirled every which way—forward, backward and sideways, then in spirals.

Snow was gusting wildly all around, and I could taste the freezing cold outside. When at last the car was still, I loosened my tight grasp on the steering wheel, but quickly realized I had no idea which direction I was facing. How did pilots get their bearings in whiteout conditions? Instruments, yes. Mine told me only that the gas tank was three-quarters full, the motor wasn't too hot or too cold, and I was travelling zero kilometres per hour.

I knew I was halfway between Blue River and Clearwater. Staying there, stationary, wasn't an option, so I put the Sidekick into second gear and continued at a painfully slow speed in the direction I hoped was south, praying to my great-grandfather, Mosom, that a huge truck wouldn't slam into me and that I wouldn't inadvertently drive off a cliff. There were no other vehicles travelling in either direction. If anything were to happen, there would be no one there to help me.

In my frantic state, I realized that recently, on a near-daily basis, I'd actually fantasized about driving off a cliff, steering into the path of a speeding eighteen-wheeler or swimming so far out into Sxstélenemx that I wouldn't be able to return to shore. My life in Salmon Arm had become unbearable. The peace and joie de vivre I'd felt while canoeing with Alex had dissipated. The white staff and consultants who had initially agreed to assist with the recruitment and hiring of Indigenous educators had recanted and become hostile. Some confronted me directly, while others had their wives, friends or even parents call me at home to protest the change in NAERC's hiring practices.

We had a team that was almost entirely Indigenous now, but new complications had arisen. I was private about my personal life to the point of appearing secretive, and this had become a problem. First, the Metis woman we'd hired to replace Ethan called late one night to say she couldn't travel with me to do a presentation in a northern college as we'd planned because her husband was convinced she and I were going away on a romantic tryst. Another day, our receptionist and part-time accountant didn't show up for work and couldn't be reached. We learned that she was in a women's shelter in Kamloops. She'd fled home because her husband had violently confronted her, accusing her of having an affair with me.

I focused on my driving. There was still no traffic in either direction, or was it just that I couldn't see it through the blowing snow? I tried to ascertain if I was driving on the right side of the road, then decided it was important to just be on the road, period. The speedometer read twenty. I hoped to come across a motel where I could rest, but there were none. My mind raced with new worries that made me tense up even more.

Alex had been hired as the adult education instructor for an off-campus college program at Neskonlith Indian Reserve, so he'd come to live with me. Within months of his taking the position, rumours reached me at the office that the men on the Neskonlith reserve were scheming to murder or maim him. They were convinced that Alex had been partying and having sex with his young female students, who were all mothers and in committed relationships. I wasn't completely surprised to hear this accusation. One Sunday afternoon I'd returned from a weekend in Vancouver to find him alone in my place with a white teenage girl named Candy. He was serenading her with "Pour Some Sugar on Me."

The storm outside was not letting up. In fact, visibility was worse than ever. But I didn't dare stop. This usually pleasant eight-hour drive along a serene and scenic route had turned into a nightmare. The temptation to floor the accelerator and veer off the road increased with every passing second. I was in a hell of my own making: I'd left Yekooche, a place where I'd had a bright future and where the locals loved me, for a job in a setting where people backstabbed each other. My bosses expected me to generate revenue for the college, but I wanted to direct NAERC's net profits toward programming for local First Nations; I'd forced Ethan out of his dream job and he was now undermining me from the sidelines, turning my boss and the new team I'd hired against me. I'd ended my love relationship with Milan to pursue Alex, but Alex didn't love me and had actually turned out to be a cad.

After five more hours of driving a distance I should have covered in two, the blizzard cleared just past the village of Chase. The blue numbers on the dashboard clock read 3:00 a.m. Half asleep, I kept driving, cautious of the patches of black ice covered by powdery snow.

Then something in the rear-view mirror caught my eye. A huge timber wolf, and it was following me. Was I seeing things? I blinked, shook my head and glanced at the side mirror. There he was, just above the words *Objects in mirror are closer than they appear*. The wolf was gaining on me. The wind whipped the particulate snow upward in swirls, and my car began to rock from side to side. When I stepped on the accelerator, the vehicle fishtailed, so I let up on the speed. The static on the radio gradually transformed back to music—k.d. lang, singing her new hit, "Constant Craving." I glanced repeatedly at the rear-view mirror to watch as the wolf blended into the scenery behind me.

❖

The drive from Salmon Arm to Vancouver was five hours long, but I often made it in four and a half, desperate to escape to the safety of caring friends, gourmet food, fine wine, encouragement, advice. Milan was ever-present and patient. Did he know? Could he see that the werewolf within me I'd worked so hard to suppress was back, and it was taking over? Could he smell its lusty odour? Did he guess that the real purpose of my solo shopping trips to Granville Street was to feed my obsession with sex? Displaced angels downtown took astonishing forms.

❖

Annie, a Nlaka'pamux co-worker at NAERC, invited me to her home near Lytton for the Labour Day weekend. Great, I thought, I'll get to spend a few days on an Indian reserve—draw closer to the people. Within hours of my arrival, some friends of Annie's came over. One man took out a skinny joint, lit it and passed it around. I didn't like to smoke pot, but I wanted to fit in, so when the joint was passed to me, I took a deep draw and held it in, trying to create the impression I was a seasoned pothead. After the joint had made the rounds a few times, I felt giddy. Yes. Now I belonged.

But a short while later, I noticed that when I took a mouthful of coffee, I didn't taste anything. Nor did I feel the liquid go down my throat. The conversation around me had become fractured. As in a faulty TV transmission, there was a time lag between the movement of people's lips and the sound coming out of their mouths. Frightened, I went to stand beside Annie, who was peeling potatoes in the kitchen.

"Darrel—everything okay? You're white as a parsnip."

I couldn't answer her, and I felt stupid staying glued to her side, so I rushed outside to sit on the grass. I knew *it* was real. I crawled under her deck, where I thought I would be safe. When I spotted a lonely phone booth across the gravel road, I thought about calling Gaylene or Milan, but I didn't want to worry them. So

I just sat there astro-travelling: one minute I was at Gaylene's house in Edmonton, lying on the couch; the next, I was in bed at Milan's place in Vancouver, pulling blankets up to my chin to keep warm.

From out of nowhere a pack of rez dogs appeared and surrounded me. At first they seemed friendly. One of them moved to lick my hand and face. Lurking in the distance I could see a timber wolf. Was it the one that had followed me the night I was driving home in the snowstorm? The wolf had an adversarial co-worker's head! Had he somehow masterminded my demise?

I had no control as I watched the scene unfold in front of me. I sobbed as the rez dogs transformed into vicious coyotes and moved in closer. Mary Thomas had told me what coyotes represent in Secwepemc culture. They're like *wihtikiw* for us Crees—shape-shifters, man-eaters, cannibals. I shouted for Mary to help me, but her name got stuck in my throat. I conjured her beautiful, tranquil face and heard her say, "I love you, Sonny." As the coyotes moved in for the kill, I blacked out.

❖

I headed back to Salmon Arm the next morning, grateful my close call hadn't been disastrous. I'd refrained from doing drugs in my youth, other than smoking pot on rare occasions, because I was so afraid of surreal experiences like the one I went through the night before—of losing control, as I had seen one of my uncles do when he tried to fly off a balcony on the seventeenth floor of a high-rise, or like Mother, the time she had tried to burn our house down, with us kids in it, in an alcohol-induced psychotic episode.

Annie didn't blame me—she thought the joint must've been laced with something. In any case, I had a splitting headache, and as I drove into Salmon Arm I stopped at the drugstore in the shopping mall to ask for advice on what might help.

The pharmacist, a tall, aging white guy, was busy chatting with someone, so I wandered over to the literature rack I spotted nearby. My jaw dropped when I got close enough to decipher the rubric *Aryan Nations—White Pride*. Propaganda published by white supremacists to advance their beliefs and cause. I glanced around. The other customers seemed normal. They were all white, but did they know about this and agree with the message? I began to rage. How could anyone get away with this in Canada? Silence was complicity.

❖

The smell of woodsmoke took me back to Mosom's trapping cabin, when I was a toddler. The dome-shaped sweat lodge, no more than five feet high, maybe ten feet in diameter, was built on a hillside overlooking Kalamalka Lake. In the heart of the firepit in front of the entry, heated rocks—crimson red grandfathers. Inside, complete darkness—solitude—even with eleven other men sitting alongside me in a tight circle. As the steam intensified, my fears and anxieties melted away. The elder sang and prayed. At last, relief from my constant torment.

In that lodge, I experienced my first visitation. Was it the intense, moist heat or the chanting of the elder that set the stage for it? It seemed the most natural thing in the world. While I didn't recognize individual spirits, I felt a powerful collective presence, and instinctively I knew it was my ancestors.

They calmed and strengthened me and gave me direction for the future: I would walk a red path, but in a way I hadn't yet seen anyone else do. I wasn't sure what that meant. I decided I'd begin doing ceremonies on my own regularly, for guidance. I knew I couldn't boast about my new life to anyone or live with the delusion that I was now somehow more spiritually evolved than others.

After the last of four steam-filled rounds, I stepped out of the lodge into daylight. Everything was so much more vivid: the turquoise-green Kalamalka Lake and her protectors, the surrounding brown hills. The lodgepole pine, Indian paintbrush, a blue jay squawking, a frenetic squirrel already preparing for winter.

❖

The next week, Emil Auger called me to say he was coming to Salmon Arm for a visit and ask if he could stay at my house. I couldn't wait to talk to him about my first sweat lodge experience. I knew he'd been to a sun dance and completed the whole ceremony, which, for me, would have been daunting.

"So," said Emil, as he entered my office holding a cup of steaming coffee. "Tell me about Trina—or is it Greg? And Diane... or is it Danny?" I felt the blood drain from my head. Suddenly I knew exactly what he was going to say next, and what I would answer, and how our conversation would end. What did that mean? I was sure it couldn't be good. It must be a warning.

I rushed to close my door and moved close to where Emil stood. I said in a whisper, "How did you hear about Greg and Danny, ahh..." My voice cracked. "Trina and Diane?" Fear overwhelmed me, paired with shame. I'd get fired, I was sure, once word got around the college about my family members—their gender transitions and Diane's dramatic suicide, her body discovered on her mother's grave, hair shorn, clad in men's clothing.

"It's a small world. Folks tell me these things, when it's about our people."

I was flustered. Now Emil had power over me. Would he abuse it or gossip about me? Would I become the laughingstock of Salmon Arm, become even more isolated than I already was?

That night, I made dinner for Emil. "Don't go putting any love medicine in my food or drink now, eh?" he said with a smirk as he stood watching me work.

So, he'd heard about me too and was making fun of me. What made him assume I was attracted to him? He was handsome with long, thick braids, but sex with him hadn't crossed my mind.

The next morning when I got up, Emil was gone.

That evening, around 6:00 p.m., my phone rang. I ran to the den to answer it. It was Emil.

"Darrel, I left my medicine bundle and pipe in your house, in the spare room. This never happens, but listen, there's a reason. You're supposed to use it to do a ceremony on your own. I'll give you instructions—write them down."

I set things up as Emil advised, in front of a blazing fire in my living room. I did everything he had told me, and within seconds, the room was filled with my ancestors. This time, I recognized most of them: Nigawi, Notawi, Auntie Helen, Cucuum Adele, Cucuum Philomene, Mosom Powder, along with others I'd never met—Mosom's grandparents, I guessed. A comforting warmth came over me.

I wondered if I should sing for them, a Nehiyaw chant like I'd heard Mosom do, but maybe it would seem fake. I'd first have to learn how to chant while beating a hand drum. Suddenly, complete calm came over me, and I knew everything would be okay. An *échappatoire* would become apparent with time.

My ancestors were still present when I went to bed. That night, I dreamed about the Pacific Ocean, over and over. First gentle, rhythmic waves, which I admired from the beach, then an enormous wall of water beneath which I was perched, precariously, on a rocky outcrop with no escape. Abruptly, I was in the water. I bobbed up and down with the swells, but I felt in control. After a few seconds, I spotted the shoreline and began to confidently swim toward it.

Some Kind of Hero

THE WOODEN PEWS and floor of St. James Catholic Church in the hamlet of Smith shook with each resounding thunderclap. Through the fake stained-glass windows, lightning bolts flashed repeatedly across our faces. Smells of second-hand smoke, bacon, Brylcreem and leather wafted in the air. My distraught family huddled together in the first two pews, while in the middle rows were the sombre faces of first, second and third cousins. At the back, in front of the confessionals, intrigued onlookers stood beside a flock of reporters who juggled pens, notebooks and cameras with obscenely long lenses. I crouched forward to clasp the hands of my sisters Gaylene and Holly. Their palms felt moist and sticky like mine. Was their debilitating fear invading me? Would a similar pathetic fate claim each of us? Who would be next? Travis had been thirty-one, the same age our oldest sister, Debbie, had been when she died a decade earlier. She didn't have this kind of farewell, but the austere Protestant ceremony, followed by a lonely interment in the middle of a vast prairie, wasn't any less painful.

Another series of blue flashes and thunderclaps. I looked up at the wooden ceiling and high windows, convinced it was Travis's spirit fomenting this dramatic departure, thrusting itself into another dimension while venting anger at our family, the church, society and me. We had all failed him. Could he now forgive me, so we could have a closeness that we hadn't had while he was alive? I sat squirming in the crowded pew, trying to understand how my brother could have authored this nightmare.

What was taking the damn priest so long? It was already 11:15, and we were supposed to have started at 11:00. My petite Auntie Rosie, now our clan mother, snuck alongside the railing in front of the altar area to get to the rectory. After another fifteen minutes, a harried Father Proulx, his black three-pointed biretta askew on his bald head, stumbled out of the sacristy and stepped up to the lectern. Auntie Rosie stood off to one side.

The priest's unsteady voice: "Dearly Belov-*h*'ed, we *h*'are gat'ered 'ere today to join..."

"No, Father, I marked the page for you," Auntie chided.

"*h*'Oh yes." He flipped heavy pages and continued, "We *h*'are gat'*ered* 'ere to bid farewell to *h*'our beloved bro'*der*, ah..."

"Travis, Father, Travis Edward."

"Yes, Trav-*h*'is... *h*'Ed*ward.* Son of Bertha D*ora* and *h*'Ed*ward.*"

I loathed the scripted ritual that was about to play out, and I was anxious about what would happen when it was over. Reporters' ruthless questions, the accusing faces of small-town strangers. The priest's voice droned on.

❖

The previous morning over breakfast in the café of a generic motel outside Hinton, I'd sat studying the lush evergreen-flocked foothills of the Rockies, dreading my return to Smith. I still didn't grasp what had happened, though my sister Gaylene had told me bits and pieces over the phone. The waitress brought my crisp bacon and eggs over easy with brown toast, topped up my coffee and set the *Edmonton Sun* in front of me. I glanced first at the date, August 5, 1992, and then scanned the front page. HIT AND RUN DRIVER HANGS SELF AFTER KILLING TWO, it read, above a blown-up mug shot of my younger brother, Travis.

I set my fork down and peered around to see who might be watching, afraid people would somehow know it was my brother at the centre of all this. Blinking back tears, I stood and strode to the bathroom. Inside a locked cubicle I rested my head in the palms of my hands. How could this be happening? Travis had killed two people and then himself?

In the bathroom's oversized mirror, I looked myself squarely in the eye, hoping I would have a few minutes to myself like that. There it was, that familiar look of devastation: my irises almost completely black, the whites covered by a network of red lines. I had been through this a few times by now, so I knew what to do—peer as deeply as I could into my own eyes and breathe. I murmured aloud, "You did what you could, Darrel. Travis and Diane lived with you for months in your little studio apartment with a view of Stanley Park. You slept on the floor so they could have the bed. You tried to get close to Travis, but your idiot brother-in-law Jim poisoned his mind against you." When someone came into the bathroom, I went silent and brushed past him out the door.

Before I got back on the road, I called Gaylene.

"It's me. You see the headlines?"

"Yes. Darrel, the phone's been ringing off the wall—reporters. Bastards. I shouldn't have bailed him out," she sobbed.

"I'm on my way."

A few hours later I pulled up to Gaylene and John's huge boxy house in the new subdivision of Castle Downs in Edmonton's north end. Salmon-coloured stucco. Nice. They had used their lottery winnings to buy their dream home. The front door flew open—a heady blend of pot and cigarette smoke. Gaylene melted into my arms.

❖

The incense filling the church brought me back to the present. As an altar boy, I had loved walking behind the priest in a cloud of fragrant smoke as he swung the brass censer from side to side while chanting in Latin. Father Proulx was doing the same thing as he staggered toward the metallic casket containing my brother Travis. The huge crucifix facing the open casket held a near-naked and bleeding Jesus. Through the haze I studied Travis's rugged face and callused hands, the fingernails chewed to stubs. He looked hauntingly like me. *But for the grace of God* leapt into my mind before I could block it. Couldn't wait to get home, away from this place, the memories and the sense of perpetual tragedy. *It's as if someone put a curse on us...* I tried to block that thought too.

At 12:45, we arrived at the graveyard. I stepped out of the green limousine into a gaggle of reporters holding small voice recorders. Is it true that he hanged himself? Who found him? Was he still alive when he was found? Are the reports accurate that he was intoxicated on both cocaine and alcohol? Was he alone in the truck during the hit and run? Was he truly your second sibling to commit suicide? How did the other one do it?

"Please, leave our family to mourn in peace. My brother is dead."

The reporters rushed over to our youngest sister, Crystal, to see if she would be the weak link. I didn't get there fast enough—a reporter in a dark trench coat asked her a question I couldn't hear, and Crystal began to blubber. I moved right in close to her. "Please, leave my sister alone. Can't you see we're in mourning?"

I glanced over at Travis's ex-wife, Diane, and their three little kids, the youngest a toddler. Beautiful, healthy children, all with

Travis's distinctive features. Thankfully the reporters didn't seem to know who Diane was.

Travis was the darkest, but he came right after the fairest one in our family, Gaylene. Their father, my stepfather, Ned, was a fair-skinned Metis, but Travis had the most Nehiyaw face of us all, and he suffered the consequences without having the cultural strengths or resources to deal with it. I had only gotten "fucking Indian" once on Edmonton's 118 Avenue, but Travis was called that every time he was thrown out of the tawdry bar on that street, which catered to Indians, downtrodden whites and a few troubled blacks. Being stopped by the cops was a regular event. In the last few years of his life, he had felt some camaraderie with his most recent best friend, our sister Holly's husband, Jim—or Relic, as Jim liked to call himself—a pothead Newfoundlander who claimed he was part Indian too, Migmaw, though he consistently spewed racial slurs against Indians, "Pakis" and anyone else who wasn't white.

Relic had coaxed Travis into a world of pot and crack, a world my brother had vehemently resisted in his teens and early twenties. Relic and I had been bitter enemies since the day I invited my sisters out to celebrate my university graduation and didn't include him, warning him to stop beating Holly or he would have to deal with me. Somehow, in spite of his caustic personality and violent behaviour, he still carried the title Uncle Relic among my nieces and nephews. I tried to reunite with Relic and Holly in the year following Travis's death. Holly and I got close again, but Relic remained indifferent. During the many days and nights I spent in their ramshackle house in Edmonton, I conjured a sequence of vignettes about Relic's relationship with Travis that I struggled without success to purge from my being:

With peanut butter glued to the roof of his mouth, Relic stuck his lips out. "I tol' her to buy smooth Kraft, not this shit," he grumbled as soon as his mouth was moist enough to move. He reached for the salt to sprinkle on his dull yellow yolks surrounded by crispy golden lace, in the process pushing over his thermal cup of steaming black coffee. "Fuck!" he yelled as he jumped up, knocking his chair over backwards. "What a fuckin' awesome day this is gonna be! Damn, six thirty already. Havta leave in ten. These fuckin' Mondays are brutal."

Relic slathered a thinner layer of lumpy peanut butter on his slightly burned toast, then took a spoonful of gooey *dulce de leche* from its glass jar and spread it over top. "I told her to buy Nutella, but instead she got me this caramel crap from Argentina. But s'posedly her brother Darrel loves it. Darrel is such a fag, trust him to bring this shit into our lives. But Travis—now he'd been a man." Relic slipped his hand down by his waist and felt for his new hunting knife in its stiff leather sheath. "Well, at least she did one thing right—best birthday present anyone ever got me."

He shoved his chair back, plopped on his pink toque and headed for the door. As he grabbed a couple of bananas and slid them into his coat pocket, his fingers brushed the ten-peso coin Darrel had given them as a souvenir of Mexico. "Fag and a cheap bastard to boot."

The powdery snow crunched under Relic's steel-toed work-boots. He watched his breath form a mist around him and felt the cold air on his cheeks.

Most of her family drove him crazy, but not Travis—they had worked together and played together. Long hours of pulling up shingles and shooting nails followed by toking and joking. Relic hated the way some of the fuckers at work goaded them—"you guys're hangin' out a lot. Ya lickin' each other's balls or what?" Fuck them, they were just jealous of how close Relic and Travis were, and if they did anything queer, well, that was between the two of them. Relic pulled himself into his crew-cab truck and stole a glance at the passenger side, where Travis usually sat when they drove to their roofing jobs. Travis had been dead for a month now. With the back of his tar-stained hand, Relic brushed away warm tears. As he shifted the truck into neutral, he thought back to his conversation with Travis hours before the cops had arrived.

"Ya idiot. They'll findja here. Yer truck's parked in the back yard, fer fuck's sake. Ya don't think anyone seen ya last night when ya ran those two chinks over? And yer an Injun ta boot. Yer gointa jail, man, for a long time. Any fuckin' idea what they'll do ta ya in jail? It's all true, ya know—all that stuff they say. Y'll fuckin' be some big tattooed guy's bitch."

Travis had leaned back in the kitchen chair, unable to speak— terror in his eyes.

"Gaylene bailed ya out, but they t'rew da book atcha, man. Hit 'n fuckin' run, DUI. Possession. Criminal neg causin' death. They're gonna fuckin' lockya up 'n t'row away da key. Be better off dead."

❖

The only time Gaylene and I sang together was when we were cruising around Edmonton in her teal Grand Am on a quest to find either books on spirituality, herbology and self-healing, or a new place to have tea. We'd just listened to her CD we'd both come to love of the Northern Cree powwow singers, and now we were wailing the chorus of "No Woman No Cry" by Bob Marley. I felt a rush of emotion when we got to the line where the lyrics asked his little sister not to shed any tears. *Mahti poni mahto nsims*, the Cree equivalent I'd just learned, popped into my head. I forced a stop to the visuals that began to flash through my mind—all the times I'd begged Gaylene not to cry, too numerous to count. I didn't want to relive them now. This was a happy time for Gaylene and me. I would be in Edmonton for a week, and we could take all the time we wanted to visit—just the two of us—and we were both in a good place. Gaylene and John were living comfortably off their lottery money, and I had a well-paid job I loved with the BC government.

Gaylene was glamorous in those days, with a feathered mid-length hairstyle that she got touched up weekly, classy artificial fingernails, delicate false eyelashes. Almost daily I asked her to pose for pictures, alone or with her daughters, Jen and Maggie.

Without warning, Gaylene pulled into the parking lot of a nondescript bar we'd never been to on 124 Street. She parked, let the song "Buffalo Soldier" play through, then butted her cigarette and pushed the button to eject the CD. Warm sunshine. Cavernous lounge.

"Oh, Darrel, it's so nice to spend time with you," she said. "You know, things have been rough lately between John and me. I'm thinking of leaving him again." Her intense blue eyes locked onto mine as we shifted our bodies to get comfortable on the swivelling bar stools. I curled my toes and clenched my jaw. Things hadn't gone well the last couple of times she'd left John, and her girls had paid the price. Her face hardened at my silent response.

"It's hard to believe it's been a couple of years since Travis died," she said.

"I know," I said. "I've thought so much about him, him and me, how much he changed in the couple of years he lived with Holly and Relic. How much he resembled me when he died. When he and Diane lived with me in Vancouver, she was so big with Travis Junior, and he was in a dark place. I tried to cajole him out of it, but after weeks of trying I gave up. I should've tried to get him help—some kind of therapy or support. At the very least, I could have told him I loved him."

Tears in her eyes and mine, but no way would we cry. Not here. We had shed enough tears together over the years—every time she, Travis and the girls were taken into foster care, after Debbie's suicide and then Mother's terminal cancer.

"His death still bothers me. Just can't get past it," she said as she put a Player's Mild up to her lips and flicked her lighter.

I felt myself stiffen, dreading what she might say next.

"I didn't want to tell anybody, but I can't hold it in anymore. You know Jen is saying he bothered her as a child. Relic, I mean."

I clenched my fists. For years I had been expecting that to come out. I'd long suspected that both of Gaylene's daughters had been abused by Relic during weekend sleepovers, but I hadn't dared say anything for fear of being ostracized like Mother had been after scolding Relic for driving drunk and stoned from Vancouver to Edmonton with Holly's son—a toddler then—in the car with him. Luckily, Holly's boy had only suffered minor injuries in the accident they'd been in. I stifled the rage welling up within me.

Gaylene drew in a puff, then exhaled a cloud of blue smoke. "You know what? Travis wasn't alone the night of the accident. Relic was with him. Travis didn't remember driving. And when he hung himself, he had help. Relic talked him into it. Helped him to set things up, to climb onto the stool, pull the noose around his neck. I bet Relic was the one who kicked the stool away. Cut Travis down with his hunting knife before the cops and paramedics got there."

My jaw dropped, and my gut tightened. Why was Gaylene rallying so fiercely against Relic? She'd always defended him, which had confused me. From the time Relic entered our lives, there had been a weird complicity between the two of them. I wasn't sure if I should believe Gaylene now. Was this some kind of caprice aimed at discrediting Relic in my eyes? If it was a ploy to make me hate him even more, it worked. I wanted to leap up and yell, to find the bastard and kill him. First, Relic had befriended and slept with my transgender sister, Trina, then he'd tried to date Gaylene. He'd moved in with Holly and beat her, turned Travis against me, molested my two sweet nieces, and now this.

I took deep breaths subtly, until I felt the pounding in my chest calm.

"How do you know all that?" I asked Gaylene.

"Relic *told* me when we were high together at their house, just the two of us, the month after Travis died. I think he expected me to thank him. Say he was some kind of hero."

I glanced around again. Good—no one was within earshot. I waved for the waitress to bring the bill, then pushed my stool back and stood.

"I'll be right back."

I locked the door of the restroom and went over to the mirror. I muttered to myself to relax, to take it easy. "There's nothing you can do unless the girls file a complaint. Jesus, did Gaylene and Holly know about the abuse the whole time? Did Relic sexually abuse Holly's boy, Jason, too? As for the questions around Travis's death, it's far too late..."

Gaylene was waiting for me beneath the red exit sign, cigarette package and lighter in hand. She popped in a different CD before putting the car in reverse: Billy Crystal's corny routine "I Hate When That Happens" began to play. Halfway through it we were bleary-eyed from laughter.

"Hate it when that happens," Gaylene echoed as she pulled up the driveway to her house.

Der Erlkönig

I F EVER THERE was a sacred place and event, this had to be it: huge ceiling beams and carved house poles of cedar, floor-to-ceiling windows looking onto luxuriant grounds. Rhododendrons, lupins and late-blooming Pacific dogwoods. I was in the Sty-Wet-Tan, the great hall of the University of British Columbia First Nations House of Learning, for the yearly Indigenous graduation celebration in my capacity as special advisor on Aboriginal post-secondary education for the BC government. The day felt surreal. I'd flown over from Victoria that gorgeous spring morning by helicopter, admiring Mount Baker, the snow-capped volcano in the distance, and saying a quiet prayer of thanks when we landed in Vancouver's Coal Harbour. Now here I was, surrounded by elegantly dressed Indigenous people of all ages, their excited voices creating a hum that filled the space.

Among the graduates were a couple of new medical doctors, a few PhDs, a cohort of thirty or so new teachers, a forester, an architect, a cluster of lawyers and a handful of alumni in more obscure disciplines. I was in love with every one of them, male and female, even though I'd never met them; they were brilliant, accomplished, determined and energetic. I knew the struggle they'd gone through to get to here, and I imagined the challenges they would face working alongside people who weren't ready to accept them as experts in their respective fields. You have to be twice as good to be considered half as competent, I often said about being an Indigenous professional working with white folks. But today I only wanted to think good things.

I glanced around the crowd that had gathered—a scrum of smiling brown faces: mothers, fathers, aunts, uncles and siblings. One of the graduates resembled my brother Travis—the same almond-shaped eyes, dark complexion and full smile. I'd only seen that much joy in Travis's eyes when he was holding his oldest son, Travis Junior, in his arms as a baby.

A female grad with long straight black hair and a reticent smile reminded me of Debbie, and beside her a fairer woman with a broad toothy smile, rays of sunshine coming out of her eyes, could have been Gaylene.

At the table where they were serving coffee and bannock, I bumped into a tall young woman in a graduation gown. I'd stubbed the back of one of her clunky high heels with the tip of my shoe. When she turned to see who had transgressed, I looked into her beautifully made-up face.

"I'm sorry. Pardon me," I offered.

"It's okay. I'm not used to these thick heels," a near-baritone voice responded.

So, an Indigenous transgender woman was graduating too. Wait, I'd heard about her. I thought about Trina—she could've been among this crowd. I remembered her graduation as a nurse from Vancouver Community College—nobody had even known she was transgender. Mother and I had felt so proud of her accomplishment: going from high-school dropout and drug addict to a nurse.

When we were kids, Debbie had wanted to be a stewardess, Trina a lawyer, me a doctor and Gaylene a nurse. I thought about my incredible struggle to get through university in the days before there were supports for Indigenous students at all and even more barriers to graduating. Now here I was at this wonderful ceremony at UBC, in an important role with a lofty title. What was different about me? I knew part of the answer to that question. I'd had Mother's powerful love and attention, as well as that of Debbie and my aunties, uncles, grandparents and older cousins, until I was seven years old. I'd been nurtured by my great-grandfather, Mosom Powder. My great-grandmother Philomene had found a way to let me know she cherished me. Basking unawares in the protective embrace of sweetgrass, sage and tree fungus, I'd been nourished by the traditional foods Mother, Mosom and my uncles and aunties harvested from the land: moose meat, bone marrow, fish-head soup, rabbit, deer, beaver, mint, red willow shoots and berries. But our home fell apart before the younger ones got to experience these things, and the older two, Debbie and Trina, had been traumatized by Father's untimely death from cancer at age twenty-eight.

A gentle hand on my shoulder brought me out of my reverie: a tall slender woman with short grey hair who was likely Cree. Her gaze locked onto mine. *"Mahti poni mahto. Astum, T'airl. Come, it's feast time. There's seafood chowder, smoked sockeye, fresh greens and blackberry pie with ice cream. Mahti mitsotan."*

❖

Dark-skinned men tapped hand drums and sang. Dancers wearing dramatic wooden masks carved in abstract animal forms shuffled around a blazing fire, bowing, swooping and turning in spirals through a smoky haze, red and black button blankets draped over their shoulders and outstretched arms. Once it all stopped, the emcee for the evening said a prayer in Hul'q'umi'num, then explained in English that we had just witnessed winter dances that very few people ever got to see—moves and masks that had never been photographed or filmed.

I was the special guest at this event put on by Malaspina University College along with the Hul'q'umi'num and Snuneymuxw First Nations in the dimly lit traditional big house on the Cowichan Indian Reserve. One dancer motioned for me to step into the middle of a circle of masked dancers. I stood quivering as an elder gently placed a blanket over my shoulders, then handed me a piece of yellow cedar carved into an eagle rattle with deep red and black grooves. As another elder explained the ceremonial significance of the rattle, deeper emotions kicked in. When the drummers, singers and dancers started up again, the emcee declared in a booming baritone voice that they had gathered to honour me for sharing with the university college the vision I'd had for a program called First Nations Arts One. It was now a proven success. Tears rolled down my face.

By the time the big house celebration was over I was ecstatic, but as I flew down the Malahat highway back to Victoria in the dark of night I became uneasy. What if the tribal leaders had known about my sexual activity, past and present—and where I'd come from—a poor family in northern Alberta—an alcoholic mother. Would they still have honoured me? And why did I always feel like an imposter?

❖

When Gaylene came to visit me in Victoria, I was overjoyed. For once there would be just the two of us—no controlling husband to demand she snip his pot into flakes for joints, no distracting daughters. For years I'd dreamed of us having time to ourselves.

She came bearing gifts: oils of lavender, clary sage, lemon, Roman chamomile and oregano, along with supplements like ginseng, evening primrose oil, Coenzyme Q10 and ginkgo biloba and a copy of *The Celestine Prophecy* by James Redfield. It had been two years since she'd had any alcohol or smoked pot and she looked great, but for some reason she couldn't let go of smoking cigarettes.

In the evenings we lazed around my apartment—reminiscing, discussing life and listening to music. I played my current favourites for her: "Calling All Angels" by Jane Siberry, Sarah McLachlan's *Fumbling Towards Ecstasy*, *Deep Forest* and a new album by the Northern Cree Singers. She loved it all.

Each night in bed I read a few chapters from *The Celestine Prophecy*, and the next morning over coffee Gaylene and I would discuss the content. I was intrigued by concepts like meaningful coincidence, living in a continuous state of loving and clearing old behaviours to become psychologically and spiritually sound, but I grew cynical toward the end of the book, where I thought Redfield attempted to cleverly lead the reader to Christianity. The belief that individuals who vibrated on a higher level would become invisible to everyone else was reminiscent of the Christian rapture I'd yearned for in my born-again youth. Still, my time with Gaylene was precious.

❖

I loved the work I got to do in my new position with the provincial government, but every day I wondered if I would have a job to report to the next day. My title was impressive, but nobody knew what I did. My only job security came from Shirley Joseph, a Wet'suwet'en woman from northern BC who was the First Nations education coordinator at Vancouver Community College. Shirley had a direct line to the deputy minister's office and the ear of a number of prominent BC chiefs. The two of us became close, speaking daily by phone or in person.

Sex remained my main stress reliever. Wherever I travelled I found willing partners to engage in frenzied intimacy, and I combined sex with alcohol until one day I went to the office so hungover I was unable to utter a coherent sentence. That scared me. I knew what it could lead to. That wasn't what I wanted in life, nor did I want to confirm that Indigenous people were drunks. For the time being, one drink became my maximum even when colleagues encouraged me to drink more.

My role with the government was challenging: convincing a committee of directors and assistant deputy ministers to fund new Aboriginal certificate and degree programs in colleges and universities. My colleagues, all white—policy analysts, economists and accountants—made the same argument: if they agreed to fund special programs for "Natives," they would have to do the same for other minorities—Chinese Canadians, South Asian Canadians, Ukrainian Canadians and so on.

Luckily, I found some allies in the ministry, and after just a month as special advisor, I'd honed my response, keeping my voice calm and my demeanour neutral. "With respect, other 'groups' aren't victims of rapid and brutal colonization, their culture and language methodically suppressed, their territory and birthright usurped, their suicide rates four times the national average, their children making up half of the kids in government care, with gross overrepresentation in prisons, a lower life expectancy than other Canadians, poor educational outcomes at all levels and low economic participation. If any minority group ever faces a crisis remotely similar to what we are facing, I hope government will seriously consider their proposals."

I didn't bother to mention the unique and important status that "Indians" were accorded under Section 35 of the Canadian Constitution, knowing that eyes would roll.

The NDP government under Premier Mike Harcourt had allocated more than six million dollars for new Aboriginal program funding, but many bureaucrats weren't supportive of this direction. To appease their concerns that much of the money would be wasted, I worked with a team of in-house economists and statisticians to design a system for measuring outcomes and impacts on Aboriginal leavers and completers in the post-secondary system. But an over-arching policy framework intended to guide my program area was long overdue, and I didn't have a clue how to bring it home. Once again, I was in over my head. I needed all the support I could get.

Strong friendships were my salvation, with Shirley Joseph, who I'd met through work; Sheila, who I knew through mutual friends; her Rotuman husband John—an Indigenous man who was a champion bodybuilder; Ted; his partner, Yolande; and Milan with his undying devotion in spite of the breakup. Sheila, the only person to tell me that I had no reason to feel inferior to my white male friends, gave me amazing advice to solve challenges at work, as did Ted. Yolande had been on the selection committee that hired me for my first teaching job twenty years earlier, and Ted had been my vice-principal and mentor—he had groomed me to become a school administrator. Early in our friendship, he encouraged me to reconnect with Cree culture and language. Once I began to tell him about travesties committed against the plains Cree and other Indigenous peoples in Canada, he began to research related topics, and we got together regularly to compare notes. Ted was generous in other ways too, giving me his seasoned canoe and the worn briefcase he had used throughout his career. And each time Ted and Yolande came to visit, Ted brought new music to share. His latest gift was a CD by Salif Keita, a Malian griot—a blend of storyteller, historian and shaman. My growing circle of Indigenous friends from different places—Marion Roze, Linda Thomas, George Littlechild, Kathy Absolon, Shelley Cardinal and Joanne and Sandee Mitchell—shared intimate details of their lives and demanded I be more forthcoming about mine.

And I started picking berries again—a seasonal activity I'd done with Mother every year from as early as I could remember. Together as a family we'd harvested gooseberries, strawberries, raspberries, blueberries and cranberries, high and low bush. Enough to preserve and share.

When I met Jo-Ann, Ethel, Madeleine and Roz, more appropriately addressed as Dr. Archibald, Dr. Gardner, Dr. McIvor and Dr. Ing, at UBC upon joining the President's Advisory Board on First Nations Education, I was taken aback by their deference and respect. They asked me to say the opening prayer for a few meetings, and before long I became the committee chair. These four empowered and accomplished Indigenous women became beacons. Did they understand where I was from—the bush of northern Alberta? But I worried endlessly. What if they were to find out about my acting out sexually, often the night before our advisory board meetings? Would they still accept me then?

On one trip to Vancouver I met one of the most beautiful men I'd ever seen—*miyowâpewiw*—tall and muscular with a smooth pecan-shell torso, enticing white smile and lively eyes. Long sleek black hair. After a couple of hours of intense passion—his large and perfect hands all over my body and my lips all over his—we held each other in a close embrace and fell asleep like that. I was smitten, but Ravi wasn't. In the morning, he told me about his arranged marriage—his young bride would soon arrive from India. He'd saved up for years for her dowry. When I got home to Victoria, I made a simple coded entry in my journal to commemorate him: *Langsat and tamarind. Cinnamon and vanilla.*

Gaylene returned for another visit and after a couple of days in Victoria we travelled to Vancouver. We went out to nice restaurants for dinner and shopped in fancy stores. But our visit was cut short when our youngest sister, Crystal, called to inform us that Ned had had a heart attack and was in intensive care. Gaylene flew back to Edmonton but Ned died hours before she arrived. Suddenly I wished I'd spent more time with Ned. I'd visited each time I'd gone to Edmonton and even though we weren't close emotionally, we respected each other. Gaylene wore the beautifully beaded knee-length buckskin shift that she'd bought on her last Vancouver trip to Ned's funeral in Smith. She arrived five minutes before the mass began. The two of us had had a falling out by that point in my trip because right after Ned died, she had started drinking and doing drugs again, following two years of abstinence. She had left John by this time and bought her own house in Edmonton, a nice three-level split. It was barely set up, but she'd furnished a guest room near the front entrance, so that's where I slept. The day we went to the funeral home to select a coffin, she invited her new boyfriend and his friends to her house. They drank, smoked pot and played loud music the rest of the afternoon and into the night. Just after midnight I left in a taxi for a nearby motel. Gaylene was furious.

The mood was tense at Ned's funeral—different than at Debbie's, Travis's and Mother's, where the family had been united by grief. Gaylene and I had sworn Travis's funeral would be the last Catholic service we subjected ourselves to, but I hadn't known what else to do—we owed it to Ned's other relatives to give him a proper funeral.

Ned hadn't been particularly religious. He believed in Indian medicine, I thought, but he never spoke about it. There were a lot of topics he didn't discuss—the war had traumatized him. He and Gaylene were very close, and from the time she was born, she brought him joy. He called her his blue-eyed Indian and he was her Papa.

After Ned's service and interment, I wandered over to where Travis and Mother were buried. My face froze when I read the epitaph on the marble gravestone Ned and Gaylene had commissioned for Mother: *Here lies Bertha Dora Villeneuve—loving mother of Gaylene, Travis, Holly and Crystal.* Where was my name, or Debbie's, Trina's? Our cousins in Smith were mystified.

Ned had been a place marker for my own father—the two of them had been close cousins. One evening long before, I had told him I planned to change my last name from McLeod to Cardinal because I felt closer to Mother's side of the family. He became irate, which was rare, and said, "If you do that I'll disown you." His response had shaken me and now I was mourning his loss.

Ned had always been there and had willingly provided for me like a son. He'd loved my sister Debbie like a daughter. He wasn't our biological parent, but somehow, he'd embodied my father, Sonny. His death made me miss my real father even more intensely. I'd stayed up all night on the eve of my twenty-eighth birthday, fearing that if I fell asleep I would die. Twenty-eight was Father's age when he died from cancer, and for years I'd been convinced I too would die young. Sleepless, I'd played a recording of "Der Erlkönig" ("The Elf King"), a Goethe poem set to music by Schubert, about a boy riding home on horseback in his father's arms. The boy becomes terrified when he is lured by the Elf King, a spine-chilling supernatural being. The boy's father cannot see or hear the mystical creature and tells the boy that his imagination is playing tricks on him. It had moved me to tears when I'd first heard it in a music appreciation class during my last year at UBC, even though the lyrics were in German. Sitting in just my underwear on the wooden floor of the house I was caretaking that summer, I played the recording over and over until morning.

Years later, I took the best English translation of the poem I could find and modified it to my liking—adding in Cree words where they seemed to fit.

Whitigo

Who rides there so late through the night dark and drear?
The Son it is, with his Father so dear;
He holds the man tightly clasp'd in his arms,
He holds him safely, he keeps him warm.

"My Father, why do you struggle, your face thus to hide?"

"Look, Son, the Whitigo is close by our side!
Do you not see him, the Whitigo, his crown and his train?"

"No Father, it's the mist rising o'er the plain.

"Come my dear Father! Please come now with me!
Many a game we will play—together, come now and see;
On our vast land, pussy willows their blossoms near,
And Mother will dress you with garments of fur."

"My Son, my Son, can you not hear
The words that the Whitigo now breathes in my ear?"

"Kîyâm, dearest Father, 'tis your fancy—it deceives;
It's the sad wind—sighing through withering leaves.

"Come, then, dear Father, will you go with me there?
Debbie will tend you with sisterly care;
Your daughter, by night, her merriment keeps,
She'll dance you, and rock you, and sing you to sleep."

"My Son, my Son, how can you not see,
The Whitigo—his daughters he has brought here for me?"

"Yes, my darling, my Father. I see it all right,
'Tis the aged grey willows deceiving your sight.

"I love you Father—your beauty, your joy!
And if you're unwilling, then force I'll employ."

"Dear Son, dear Son, he seizes me fast,
The Whitigo, the Whitigo—he has hurt me at last."

The Son now gallops, with terror—half mad,
He grasps in his arms his poor shuddering dad;
He reaches his tipi with toil and with dread,
His Father in his arms—is motionless—dead.

When I got back home from attending Ned's funeral in Smith, I unpacked my suitcase and then quickly repacked it with different clothes. The next day I would travel to Mexico City to participate in a cultural exchange between Mexico and Canada. I made sure the speech I'd laboured over in Spanish was easily accessible in my briefcase so I could study it on the flight.

A Copse of Maples

E SIZED ME up as I stepped into the elevator, a caged animal trying to determine if I was there to kill him. Why would he fear diminutive me, when he had two hulking armed security agents beside him and I had my red LEADER LIAISON credential hanging around my neck? We were in Vancouver for the 1997 Asia-Pacific Economic Consortium. He was Ernesto Zedillo, the president of Mexico, and I was a federal negotiator on assignment to be his liaison with the Government of Canada.

Appetizer: Smoked dick, the menu read. It was hard for the representative from the Prime Minister's Office, who was leading a walk-through of the first state dinner, to quell the boisterous laughter that had started as an isolated snicker after someone pointed out the typo. We were exhausted after three days of 6:00 a.m. briefings with bomb-sniffing dogs and their handlers shuffling around the venue, protocol lessons, role plays. We, the leader liaisons, all had to wear business attire, while the young man from the PMO, Jean Carle, cavorted in blue jeans and a white

T-shirt. I felt twinges of resentment at each pinch of the size-16.5 collar of my white shirt and my tight black oxfords.

I had debated walking out—quitting—as we were rehearsing the leaders' banquet in the large glass sunroom built specifically for the occasion at UBC's president's residence. My counterpart, the Canadian liaison to the Chinese president, had just had a meltdown about the writing implements provided for the signing of the declaration. Apparently the Chinese leader would require a brush, not a fountain pen—anything less would be insulting and a breach of protocol. Jean Carle looked out at the expansive view of the Strait of Georgia and Grouse Mountain and indicated, by a sweep of his arm, a copse of maple and arbutus trees—crimson leaves and ochre-coloured bark that had begun to peel: "Those trees have to go—they're obstructing the view." The UBC official grimaced, then scratched the order into his notebook.

Why had I agreed to do this job? Was it to move closer to my dream of becoming a foreign services officer? I recalled the animated phone conversations I had had with friends after I was selected for the leader liaison role, careful what I said because the calls were likely wiretapped. An RCMP officer had warned me this was part of the high-level security clearance process. I resented that and the questions on the form, so intrusive: Where have you lived in the last ten years? Who are you in a relationship with? Where are your family members? What is your debt load? Your religion?

I had never been so wired for comms—a cellphone with two lines, an earpiece attached to a powerful walkie-talkie radio and a fail-proof pager. My first dramatic radio call came from the accreditation centre. A man claiming to be a Mexican general was demanding accreditation though he had no credentials with him. Nobody from the Mexican delegation was answering; the man was irate. Could I please come?

As I approached, I saw the man pacing in the secure glass cubicle in full uniform, less the cap. He was a bit taller than I was, early fifties, impeccably groomed. I stepped in to greet him and say I would see what I could do to help, but the expression on his face silenced me. He gave me a brisk once-over, then stepped in so close I could taste his acrid breath and feel globules of moisture from his mouth land on my cheeks. He forced the words through gritted teeth: *"Oye güey, si no me dejen ingresar en quince minutos—parto tu madre."*

"No trabajo para ustedes señor el general, ni soy Mexicano." I turned my back without saying another word, incredulous that he'd called me *güey*—ox—and threatened to hurt me if I didn't get him in within fifteen minutes. I could almost feel his hands around my throat as I stepped up to the accreditation clerk's glass window, trembling. "I'll call the ambassador—that's the best I can do. I can't authorize his entry."

I was covered in goose skin as I walked back to the Hotel Vancouver. How had the man come to wield so much personal power and self-importance? How many people might he have killed? Would he have slain me had we been on his turf?

The next morning, it was the general's turn to tremble. I spotted him in the official receiving line between the hotel and the limousines. This time his military cap was on, perfectly positioned. Pewter and brass medals dangling from colourful ribbons covered his puffed-up chest. As he saw me step out of the revolving door to the flash of cameras and the blinding lights of TV cameras, he blanched. I was at President Zedillo's side, and I knew what was going through the general's mind. Surely only a very powerful man, good or bad, could be that close to the president, and the general had humiliated me. After a rush of pride at his look of terror, I grasped my actual role in the charade. I was a decoy, a pawn placed in front of a king to provide safe passage and be a bullet screen *le cas échéant*. Zedillo and I were inside the security box mandated by international law: two armed Canadian security agents in front of us, two armed Mexican security agents behind us.

The following day I met with the army squadron assigned to me. Twenty or so young soldiers leapt to their feet and saluted when I was introduced. "Greetings, Mr. McLeod, sir." I felt myself blush. All these virile young men were looking to me for direction. I tried to remember military scenes I had seen in movies and on television to muster a response. "At ease, soldiers," I said meekly. "Please call me Darrel."

"YES, SIR, DARREL, SIR," in unison as they saluted again.

What was I supposed to do with twenty soldiers? How would I keep them busy and out of trouble?

I was thankful, though, for the bit of comic relief. I had sunk into a funk, partially from sleep deprivation; the early-morning briefings and late-night drinks with senior security officials in their hospitality suite were taking their toll. And I was disgusted at the opulence of the decor and the food.

During our two weeks of training the food had been tasty and abundant, but now the tables in the hallways were covered by monstrous bouquets of exotic flowers, mountains of sliced tropical fruit and gigantic oval trays of brioches, almond-filled croissants, chocolate eclairs and fancy pastries I had never seen before. Carafes held gourmet coffee, designer teas and freshly pressed juices. As I went with Zedillo from event to event, I was increasingly aware that I was on the wrong side of the security perimeter. I should have been in the streets with the people protesting the presence of Indonesia's President Suharto in Canada and the fact that upholding human rights—including Indigenous rights—and combatting poverty weren't being addressed in any way at APEC. I slipped my credentials inside my trench coat when leaving or heading back to the security perimeter, but I was sure my three-piece suit gave me away—I was working with the privileged side. I didn't understand why the situation had to be so polarized. Why wasn't there a process for the protesters to communicate their legitimate concerns directly to the leaders? Why was there no involvement in the meetings of what diplomats like to call "civil society"?

For the next phase of the event—the first individual photo op for the leaders—I had to hustle over to the huge escalators of the convention centre part of Canada Place. My job was to direct President Zedillo onto the up escalator and his bodyguard onto the down escalator. I got there on time, but Zedillo's tall and hefty *escolta* balked when I motioned for him to descend. "*Mi jefe. Voy con mi jefe.*"

"*No, amigo,*" I corrected him. "*Usted tiene que bajar de este lado.*"

"*Como? Quien manda aqui?*" he demanded. As he stepped forward to follow the president, I stepped in front of him; his damp armpit was just above my nose.

"*Yo. Yo le digo.*" I extended my arm to reinforce the direction.

Like an enraged *toro* uncertain about what to do with the chihuahua nipping at his heels, he sniffed the air, then lowered his head to look down at me and burst out laughing. "*Usted?* Ha ha ha. *Está bien pues. Ya voy.*"

Late that evening, while sipping Scotch with Rick, the RCMP superintendent assigned to our delegation, I heard about an incident with President Zedillo's wife that had occurred in the afternoon. Her staff had second-guessed protocol and tried to slip her into the downtown core in a rented car under the radar. "Those idiots," Rick said. "As the president's wife, she's an internationally protected person. At a routine security check on the Granville Street Bridge, the police patrol panicked when they realized who she was. They closed the bridge in both directions. We had to send a proper motorcade to get her and their nineteen-year-old son."

"You think that's bad," another agent piped up. "A few hours after they arrived, Zedillo's agents showed up with a prostitute— an elegant, foxy one, mind you—for the son. He was pissed that he couldn't go out on his own because of his IPP status and had demanded they get a nice Canadian girl to dine with him and spend the night."

Laughter and head-shaking all around.

I watched the eleven o'clock news in my room. The protests were constant around the city, with pockets in different locations. Their main target was Suharto, but people were also protesting China's presence—the horrible human rights records of both countries. The protests were peaceful for the most part, but every now and then a small group would attempt to breach the security fence. The animosity between police and protestors was intensifying. I lay in bed reviewing all the things I had seen that disturbed me, like the secret bilateral meetings between the presidents and prime ministers and the CEOs of multinational corporations. Why was this part of the agenda not public?

With each passing day, the extravagance troubled me more. Hundreds of homeless people, largely Indigenous, had been relocated from the downtown core temporarily, with no real plans to help them. They would be eating in church-sponsored soup kitchens not far away. I thought about my own family—how we had spent the first five years of my life in my great-grandfather's trapping cabin with no electricity or running water and lived off the land. My sisters and dozens of cousins in Smith and Slave Lake still struggled to get by. Many First Nations communities lived in abject poverty, twenty people to a two-room shack with no running water. Yet here I was dressed in a Strellson suit every day, hobnobbing with government leaders, dining on gourmet food and appearing in the daily news at President Zedillo's side. Was dealing with the underprivileged populations of member economies not a key development objective of APEC? How could things truly advance without the leaders addressing this? One thing comforted me. Gail Sparrow, chief of the Musqueam First Nation, on whose unceded territory the University of British Columbia is located, was scheduled to address the leaders during their dinner in the new atrium.

Nobody was protesting Mexico's presence at the APEC summit, yet I knew from my Mexican friends about the level of corruption there. Something else disturbed me about working with the Mexican delegation. I didn't see any of the beauty, charm, camaraderie or joie de vivre I had experienced while travelling in Mexico. The petty corruption at this summit—diplomatic attachés selling event tickets intended for senior diplomats to mid-level officials who wanted the most prestigious location possible (close to the president), only to make the Mexican delegation look like a primary class playing musical chairs when the legitimate seat holders showed up; the constant phone calls and intimidation by Mexican functionaries who thought I could give them access to the president—was annoying. But there was something more, something much bigger that troubled me, though I couldn't readily grasp what it was.

One afternoon while President Zedillo was in meetings, Daniel, the senior foreign affairs officer assigned to my team, invited me for a drink in the lounge of the nearby Méridien Hotel. We were sipping our red wine, chatting in French and laughing, when we had a chilling realization. The place was filled with men in suits, and everyone except us was wearing either a green or red lapel pin. The red pins identified Canadian security agents and the green pins foreign agents. Both signalled that the wearer was carrying a concealed weapon. Daniel and I were the only two who weren't armed and authorized to kill. We were puzzled and upset. Where was the threat? Why was this level of militarization necessary in 1997 in Canada, inside a zone that had been entirely secured?

In addition to sharing nightcaps in their hospitality suite, I had coffee and lunch often with my new friend, Rick from the RCMP, and his counterpart Val, a superintendent from the Vancouver City Police. I was astonished by their ability to read people's appearances and mannerisms. "That one's packing— something big, but definitely legit," Rick said as a tall man in a grey overcoat walked by. "That one's dealing, but no time to nail him now. The guys on the beat'll catch him soon enough."

On the fourth night, around ten o'clock, Rick, Val and I were chatting about the day's events in their hospitality suite. We could hear the throngs of protesters outside on Robson Street and around the Hotel Vancouver shouting, "Suharto has got to go. Down with Suharto."

"There are more of 'em than ever tonight," Rick said, shaking his head. "They're not budging, and we can't do anything about it unless they get violent."

"There is the usual handful of professional protestors from the US and Europe who want to escalate things, but the majority are peaceful—no breaches," Val shrugged.

Right then a call came over Rick's radio.

"The bastards are on the roof!" He leapt to his feet and dashed out the door with Val on his heels. I stayed put. How could protestors have gotten up to the roof with the incredible security contingent downstairs?

A half-hour later, Rick and Val reappeared looking stressed.

"What the hell happened?" I asked.

Rick leaned in. "This can't get out, but Suharto's men were on the roof. Eight of them in sniper positions. High-powered rifles aimed at the crowd, waiting for a breach. It was a shouting match through a translator, but we convinced them to fuckin' back off— to trust us to do our job."

The next day, the scenic campus of UBC, my alma mater, had been transformed into a war zone. Mobs of young protestors were pushing up against the provocative cement and metal fence that marked the security perimeter as poorly equipped RCMP officers tried to repel them. Rumours were rampant: Suharto won't come to this key event—he won't sign the declaration or participate in the final summit photo unless protestors are cleared before he arrives; the chief from Musqueam has refused to have her speech vetted by the PMO, so she won't get to speak; there's been a security breach and protestors have taken over a section of the motorcade route; police are scrambling—might use tear gas, pepper spray or rubber bullets.

As I walked into the spacious glass atrium I noticed right away that the stand of trees Jean Carle had ordered removed was gone. Jean Carle appeared, wearing a very expensive suit and shoes some speculated were Gucci, but he wasn't his usual cocky self. He was pacing and growling into his phone. "We need them cleared now. I don't give a fuck—just do it. Push back the perimeter so the cameras can't catch both them and the motorcade in the same clips."

Word spread that Chief Sparrow's speech to the APEC leaders had indeed been cancelled.

The closing gala took place in an enormous ballroom at Canada Place. That night, my emotions were all over the map. I was past burnout after two weeks of early-morning briefings with the president's chief of staff and the security team, as well as being on call day and night. The invitation from Prime Minister Chrétien for me to join the Canadian delegation at the final event was a surprise—I had studied the gold lettering on the bluish-white card in disbelief.

The food at the gala was exquisite. I savoured each course along with its perfect wine pairing—white, red, then fizzy—but the moment that brought me both ecstasy and overwhelming guilt came when I heard for the first time, live, Canada's new young jazz sensation, Diana Krall—her swing-style jazz piano and silky voice. Next, I was transported by the esoteric gymnastics of Cirque du Soleil. My god, what was *I* doing there? I could hear my mother's voice and that of my stepfather, Ned, at once proud and dismayed: *Wah wah,* who'dja think y'are, *h'*anaways, playing big shot, dressed up fancy and being with all them important *pee-pulz*? *Wah't-stag'ats.*

I gulped. I had worked hard for this reward, and I was going to enjoy it. I didn't get to linger in my bliss, guilt and confusion for very long, either. The Mexican ambassador to Canada called my cellphone fifteen minutes into the show and at fifteen-minute intervals afterwards, saying the same thing each time: "*Le gusta el show, Darío? Por que estoy sentada tan lejos del Señor el Presidente? No me puede cambiar el asiento? Aún es posible, sabe.*" I was livid, but I couldn't ignore her calls. I'd lobbied the APEC office to get her a seat close to the president, and that was all I could do without breaching protocol, yet even after the gala had begun she was pressuring me to change her seat.

I left the event awestruck from the extravaganza, wishing I was as musically accomplished as Diana Krall or had a body of pure muscle that could fly through the air unscathed. The heavy thinking would wait until the next day when, still exhausted, I pondered again how governments collaborated at the international level with giant corporations to maximize the profits that flowed into private hands. If they could do that to bolster unfathomable wealth, why couldn't they do the same to combat extreme poverty?

I can't claim now to have had any premonitions about the massacre of Indigenous people that would take place in Acteal, Chiapas, on December 22, a month after the APEC summit, under President Zedillo's watch. The perpetrators, a paramilitary group called Máscara Roja, would never be brought to justice. But when I read about it happening, I understood what had been bothering me most about working with the Mexican delegation in Vancouver. The injustice faced by Indigenous people in Mexico was exponentially worse than that in Canada, yet the delegation I had spent so much time with ignored the issues altogether. People had vehemently denied having Indigenous ancestry themselves, even though I was sure they had caught me wistfully admiring their striking Mayan, Aztec or Zapotec profiles as we worked or socialized.

I vowed to boycott Mexico as a traveller until its government had begun a process of reparation and reconciliation with the Indigenous peoples of Chiapas.

Nisgalande

THE LETTER I'D been awaiting for eight and a half years finally came: Indian and Northern Affairs Canada had responded to my application to be registered as an Indian. I ripped it open, read it, then fell into my chair and sobbed in angered disbelief at what the bureaucrats had concluded.

> Dear Mr. McLeod:
>
> Thank you for your Application for Registration under the Indian Act received on January 21, 1991.
>
> From the information you have provided on your application, I have been unable to identify any one of your relatives in our records as having been recognized as Indians in Canada.

I called Trina to see if Indian Affairs had responded to her application, which was an exact replica of mine with identical documentation. I left a message on her answering machine. The next day Trina faxed the letter she'd received to my office. It had the same date as the letter they had sent me. After reading the first two paragraphs I was gobsmacked:

Dear Ms. McLeod:

Thank you for your Application for Registration under the Indian Act received on January 21, 1991.

From the information you have provided, I have been able to determine that your maternal grandmother is deemed entitled to be registered under section 6(1) (f) of the Indian Act. Your mother is entitled to be registered under section 6(2) of the Indian Act as she has only one parent who is entitled to registration under section 6(1) of the Indian Act.

In reference to your registration, there is no provision in the Indian Act to allow for the registration of a person when one of the parents is entitled to be registered under section 6(2) and when the other parent is not an Indian as defined by the Indian Act or is not identified.

I would have to continue living with the shame of being a "non-status Indian." Then rage about Mother's status. All her life she was proud of being Nehiyaw—official recognition by the government would've meant so much to her. But they knew exactly where to cut it off—at the threshold where any living person could benefit from it, based on the Indian Act. And they knew that because I was now a federal treaty negotiator, working for them, I wouldn't dare pursue my case in an adamant way.

Besides, I needed to be more focused than I had ever been. I'd just been promoted to interim senior negotiator of treaties for Vancouver Island, and I felt everyone was watching—waiting for me to make a misstep or fail. The Nisga'a Final Agreement, Canada's first modern land claim and treaty with the indefatigable Nisga'a Nation, was close to becoming a reality, and it was making headlines. Everybody wanted a piece of the action, and for self-serving reasons.

The Nisga'a had made the news more than a century earlier when their leaders paddled over five hundred nautical miles in an open cedar canoe from the Nass River to the Inner Harbour of Victoria to request a treaty, only to be turned away by the premier of British Columbia, William Smithe, a youngish Englishman with a high forehead, a delicate angular nose and an odd gaze: his left eye skewed inwards. Imagine their trip home, paddling the daunting distance through swells, waves and rapids, returning frustrated and empty-handed.

What had compelled them to make that journey? Was it the strange men showing up with guns and peculiar instruments to lay claim to their homeland in the Nass Valley, a place brimming with fish, trees, wildlife and minerals? Their powerful chief, Israel Sgat'iin, had ordered warriors to escort the reeking, unshaven men off their lands, but the authority of distant governments, first in London, then in Victoria and Ottawa, gave these men permission to return and return again, until they had axes and saws hacking at huge ancient trees and picks and drills penetrating the ground for gold.

The Nisga'a didn't give up. They lobbied government after government, and when that failed they took their case to court. Canada initiated negotiations with them in 1976. In 1990, the province of BC realized it had no alternative but to join in. A decade later, Premier Gordon Campbell would be in the bizarre situation of suing himself in *Campbell v. BC*, attempting to prove that the Nisga'a Treaty would create a new "order of government" and was therefore unconstitutional.

Now, after twenty-three years of mind-numbing negotiations, agreement had been reached on almost everything: fisheries, forestry, health, social services, dispute resolution and the powers of the future Nisga'a Lisims Government. But one huge obstacle remained: before it could become law, the two hundred and fifty–page agreement, and another five hundred or so pages of technical appendices, had to be translated into French. I volunteered to work on the translation and ended up being assigned to lead the process, along with Sylvain DuBois, a lawyer with a master's degree in French.

While everyone else seemed to want a stab at glory—their moment in the sun—I simply wanted to work with the Nisga'a. In particular, I wanted to work with their confident and charismatic leader, Joseph Gosnell. The Nisga'a had managed to keep their language and culture alive against phenomenal challenges, like the death of more than two thousand of their tribe members because of a volcanic eruption in the late 1700s and the loss of over half their population through introduced disease, colonization and cultural oppression. Despite all of this, the Nisga'a unceasingly sought to reinvigorate their traditional ways of governing—their *Ayuuk*.

On a Sunday night in February 1999, I checked into the Pan Pacific Hotel in Vancouver's Coal Harbour, a five-star hotel that would be my home for the time the translation project took. I tested the plush king-size bed and elegant accoutrements, looked out the huge picture windows at Burrard Inlet and the sparkling lights atop Grouse Mountain and thought about the contrast between these accommodations and those during my one trip in the early nineties to New Aiyansh, the largest of the four Nisga'a villages: a room with a single bed in the home of a Nisga'a fisherman. I had been awestruck then by the beauty, intelligence and determination of the people, by their food—we had a feast of half-dried eulachon, salmon, halibut, herring eggs on kelp and fry bread—by their discreet generosity and by their vigour. And by the captivating landscape: the Nass River, the K'alii Aksim Lisims, surrounded by jagged white, blue and grey peaks.

I had made the trip from Terrace to New Aiyansh to meet with the board of directors of Wilp Wilxo'oskwhl Nisga'a to discuss their vision for their institute and its existing post-secondary education programming back when I was the BC government's special advisor. We'd flown along the road there, the aging Father McKenzie and I, in his red pickup truck. He had been the Anglican priest in that region forever, and he must have thought God was truly with him as he gripped the steering wheel at ten and two and accelerated over the one-lane snow-packed road. Immediately to our right was a rock wall. To our left was a cliff that dropped into a lake of black lava neatly blanketed by snow and ice. I didn't know if *he* was praying, but I was—fervently. And not to Jesus, though I may have uttered his name a few times.

❖

It was a typical Vancouver winter as we set out to work on the translation. Most days we were surrounded by a dense grey mist, but on the thirty-fifth floor of the Scotia Tower we were occasionally above the clouds, giving us a clear vista of the snow-capped peaks of the coastal mountains and the dark waters of False Creek and Burrard Inlet.

My first senior officials' meeting with the Nisga'a and the provincial teams was disappointing, because Joseph Gosnell did not attend. During a break, as everyone chattered around me, I flipped through an article about him. Gosnell was born to make history—he and another Nisga'a leader, Frank Calder. Calder was twelve years old when the federal government passed a law forbidding Indians from hiring lawyers to pursue their claims and forbidding lawyers to represent them. When this changed in 1967, Frank Calder, the first Indigenous person to graduate from the UBC law school, began the long quest to take the Nisga'a's recognition of their rights all the way to the Supreme Court of Canada. Through it, he revolutionized how Aboriginal rights are dealt with in Canada. The Nisga'a lost on a technicality (they had failed to ask the federal government for permission to bring a case forward against one of its branches, the attorney general), but the court ruled that Aboriginal title still existed and that the British Royal Proclamation of 1763 still carried the force of law. While the main purpose of the Royal Proclamation was to assert ownership over former French lands, including French-speaking Quebec, the document recognized the tribes of North America as nations, acknowledging their title to their lands and strictly forbidding any settlement of them by others.

The Nisga'a Final Agreement had already been translated twice by two different contractors, but both versions had been rejected by the bilingual scholar and the law firm the Nisga'a had contracted. (They had hired big guns: a university professor and a high-profile lawyer who had negotiated billion-dollar deals for Hydro-Québec.) My bosses, Doreen Mullins from the Federal Treaty Office and John Watson from Indian Affairs, decided to cobble together a team to bring the process in-house, but they couldn't have foreseen the resistance we would experience from all sides.

By the time Sylvain and I arrived, all civility had long since gone out the window in the translation process. The lead lawyer for the BC government sat next to the counsel for the Nisga'a. The two of them took turns standing, yelling and pounding the wooden surface of the large boardroom table, punctuating their speech with "fuck" and "goddamn" and launching attacks against me, their new target, and the senior negotiator who had stoically led the federal side of the Nisga'a negotiations for years. The

Nisga'a representatives swore too, and wore scowls so deep I was convinced it would be a challenge for them to ever smile again.

When our boss, John Watson, showed up, things got even more intense.

"This is fucking outrageous, John. Why can't you just seek an exemption to the Official Languages Act and be done with it?" the Nisga'a counsel yelled.

"John, the federal government needs to foot the bill for this flawed process. I can't believe we have to renegotiate this entire treaty over again in French. You guys know goddamn well that both the English and the French versions will have equal force of law, and your people keep trying to slip things in that alter what we have agreed to," the BC government lawyer bellowed.

"If we did seek an exemption, the Final Agreement would never be fucking approved," John replied through gritted teeth. "The government house leader is a Quebec MP, a francophone; he's not going to struggle through it in English. You know that."

Good, I thought. John was matching their intensity.

Sighs and looks of dismay. Everyone would have wanted a more expeditious solution, but we were stuck in the tortuous process of creating a document in precise legal French that, once final, would be of little interest or use to anyone. For the Nisga'a, it was the ultimate insult.

"Who is this new minion, John? What can he possibly do for us?" the Nisga'a counsel asked, waving his hand in my direction.

"Oh, we've heard of him. A bleeding-heart shit disturber—what is he doing here?" demanded the BC government lawyer.

"Darrel is one of our senior negotiators, and he is fluent in French. He also has a knack for getting things done," John said as he sat taller in his chair, red patches on his pasty white face and throat.

I thought of Jean-Paul Sartre's play *Huis Clos* (sometimes translated as *No Exit*) and Sartre's notion that the "other" can condemn, define or withhold love from us and squelch our power to live as we wish, even kill us.

In Sartre's play, the characters Inèz, Estelle and Garcin, who have died and gone to hell, are locked in a room together. There were three parties in this room, too: the Nisga'a, BC and Canada. The historical relationship between them was as antagonistic as that between the characters in *Huis Clos*. This Final Agreement would allow the Nisga'a to restore their traditional ways and benefit from the lands and resources that rightfully belonged to them. As in *Huis Clos*, it wasn't possible for them to extricate themselves from this three-way relationship, but at least now the behaviour of the others would be legally defined, and where there was conflict, there would be a process of resolution and redress. The treaty would have the protection of the highest law in the land, the Constitution of Canada. Legally defined eternity.

The "no exit" aspect of Sartre's play had continued to disturb me each time I thought back to it over the years. It ran contrary to a principle my mother and Mosom, my great-grandfather, had tried to instill in me: try as they might, others cannot kill our spirit.

I glanced out one of the giant windows of the Scotia Tower just in time to see two seagulls dive-bombing a bald eagle. The eagle was headed toward a vent on the rooftop of a neighbouring high-rise where a few baby seagulls were nestled. I couldn't see how many chicks there were, but they were too young to flee. As the eagle swooped down and grabbed one in its talons, an adult seagull dove toward it to no avail. I wanted to call the others to come and look, but I didn't dare.

Why did the lawyers for the Nisga'a and the province want to prolong the translation process even further? Their behaviour was bizarre, but they knew Sylvain and I were their captive prey. I was offended daily, if not hourly. I convinced myself that they were attacking the federal system, and more specifically the faceless

French legal drafters, vicariously through me. Nevertheless, the animosity that flowed in three directions burned the phone lines running the 4,300 kilometres to federal government offices in Hull, Quebec.

Why did I stay?

I wish I could romanticize things and say I was fighting for justice and the rights of the most vulnerable party, but instead, it was my ego. In addition to wanting to ingratiate myself with the mighty Nisga'a, I wanted to spar with the big boys and show them that without stooping to their level, I could meet any challenge they threw at me and produce positive results. Mother's melodic voice sometimes played in my head. "Don't let anyone make you believe they are better than you," she'd said the day I ran home at age six with a bloody nose after Mannie, a neighbourhood bully, punched me. Instead of rushing to coddle me, as I had expected, Mother yelled, "You have to fight your own battles—I can't fight them for you. Get back out there. *Pagamahow!*"

❖

The Nisga'a were adamant that the word *Nisga'a* be capitalized wherever it appeared in the translation.

"We cannot capitalize words that are adjectives. When the word *Nisga'a* is a proper noun in French, fine, but when it modifies a noun, we cannot capitalize it," a federal lawyer insisted nasally in refined Québécois French. "This goes against basic French grammar, let alone drafting conventions, and will be off-putting for the francophone analysts and MPs who have to go through it all. They will simply reject the agreement a priori and accuse us of sloppy work. It cannot be done."

These teleconference discussions took place completely in French, so I had to listen carefully to follow the legal jargon. Sylvain and I were the proverbial meat in the sandwich between the tripartite main table and the French legal drafters for the

Department of Justice in Hull. The process stalled for at least a week as Sylvain and I debated capital *N*s and *T*s, first with the francophone lawyers to define the official federal position, then with the Nisga'a and provincial teams.

To our astonishment, one day the francophone lawyers were upbeat, convinced they had a solution to the capital *N* and *T* issue: we would call Nisga'a Lands *Nisgalande* instead of the name chosen by the Nisga'a, *Terres Nisga'a*. Sylvain and I balked at taking the idea to the table, but later decided it would be good for two things: as comic relief and to gain sympathy for the two of us. Surely the Nisga'a and provincial teams, once they realized what we were dealing with, would soften.

When we made the proposal later that morning, reminding everyone that there were countries like *Irlande*, *Finlande* and *Hollande*, so why not *Nisgalande*, there was at least five minutes of uproarious laughter.

Another morning, Sylvain, a Vancouver-based bilingual federal lawyer, and I slumped around the small hexagonal table anticipating our daily thrashing from the lawyers in Quebec. Our bellies were as bloated as our eyes were puffy. Kaila, our assistant, had kept us going through the sixteen-hour days with lamb tikka and pakoras, sushi and gyoza, gourmet pizza and Caprese salad, pad Thai and green coconut curry, enchiladas and burritos—whatever we requested, along with mounds of French pastries and coffee for breakfast. Sylvain, in his elegant French, gently told *les Maîtres* about the Nisga'a leaders' blatant rejection of *Nisgalande*. I followed up by suggesting the legal drafters simply accept the capital *N* in *Nisga'a* wherever it appeared.

I was staring at the floor, dazed from lack of sleep and too many cups of coffee, when the attack came, an infuriated male voice over the speakerphone: *"Je ne vais pas accepter qu'un criss d'anglophone à l'autre bout du pays me dise comment rédiger mon texte."* I bolted upright—now they had crossed the line.

Silence. Flushed faces. Sylvain, through stiffened lips, reminded the French lawyer that the *cris d'anglophone* they were referring to—me—had an advanced degree in French language and literature and was a senior negotiator in government. In our debrief immediately afterwards with Doreen, I translated what the lawyer in Hull had said: "I will not allow a fucking anglophone on the other side of the country to tell me how to draft my text." Doreen was incensed. She picked up the phone and motioned for us to leave the room.

The next day a francophone assistant deputy minister from the Department of Justice arrived in Vancouver. After Doreen and I had briefed him on the incident, he didn't hesitate. "You can have all of the capital *N*s and capital *T*s you want, Darrel," he said. *"Je regrette beaucoup ce qui c'est passé."*

❖

That petty issue was resolved, but the next day there was a new crisis that had nothing to do with either French grammar or legal convention. Our co-op student, a young woman with fiery red hair who had been helping us with logistical details like document management, had completed her term and been replaced by a young man.

"What have you done with Marie-Joie?" the counsel for the Nisga'a demanded. "Just when we get used to working with someone, you take them away. She was incredibly helpful to us, and we won't proceed until she is back."

With a smirk on his face, the BC government lawyer agreed. "Marie-Joie was a real asset to the federal team—your only saving grace. We won't continue our work until she's back."

The next day, with the young woman's term extended, we faced a more substantive issue. A short, dandruff-covered federal lawyer with wire-rimmed spectacles came to the main table with an unforeseen complication that had nothing to do with the translation: "The Department of Justice has been deliberating this matter at length, and we've concluded that Her Majesty the Queen in Right of Canada cannot be bound on Nisga'a lands."

Was this a joke, some kind of weird S&M fantasy of tying up the Queen, crown and all?

"Simply put," the lawyer continued, "the federal government will not allow itself to be limited by Nisga'a law on Nisga'a lands given that no province, city or town can restrict federal activities in any way in their respective jurisdictions."

The BC government lawyer exploded. "The province has already agreed that Her Majesty in Right of the Province will be bound by Nisga'a laws on Nisga'a lands, based on your word that you were going to follow suit, and now you're saying the feds can do whatever the hell they want. We've had this conversation, and clearly, for matters of national interest, like national defence, navigable waters or health and safety, the federal government can do what it needs to do. But a blanket statement like that is not acceptable."

I was confused. Were there two Queens now, two Crowns— one federal and one provincial, kind of like the holy trinity, the Father, Son and Holy Ghost? My mind was capable of abstraction, but magic realism seemed out of place here. The same federal lawyer was patient in explaining the distinction to me on a break, but I wondered how many Canadians knew about this dual nature of the Crown. At a gut level, it didn't wash with me. Nor did it with the Nisga'a, who through their lawyer brought things back down to earth. The issue was settled within a week, but the translation process had become even more acrimonious. Now there was unbridled hatred directed at anybody who worked for the federal government except our assistants.

I had begun to wonder if I was indeed working for the "evil" side, as the lawyers for the BC government and the Nisga'a had intimated. What kind of country would have two British queens who didn't want to be bound, and allow a team of federal lawyers who had likely never travelled West to hold ransom for capital *N*s and *T*s a historic deal that was worth over 196.1 million in 1999 dollars and concerned 2,019 square kilometres of land, turning it all into an Anglo-Franco political football game?

❖

The next day began with a statement from the Nisga'a French legal team: "We intend to examine every comma and every period of the translation." Sylvain and I sighed—we would be there forever. They were making success unattainable. Why was the team trying to sabotage the process and thwart the agreement that the Nisga'a had sought for over a century? The following day, a Sunday, the answer became clear. It wasn't the Nisga'a per se— it was their hired guns who had an interest in prolonging the process.

The three teams convened. The province had sent two representatives. A bilingual lawyer and I represented the federal government and supervised five teams working in the back rooms. The Nisga'a team showed up with two Nisga'a representatives, three lawyers, three accountants and their advisors. The lead provincial representative was livid, as was I. Ten minutes into the meeting we called a break and huddled.

"Do you realize what they're doing here, Darrel, how much they will be billing the federal government for all of those people?" the lead provincial representative protested. "On a Sunday their rates are double. *Ka-ching ka-ching.* If you'll walk, I'll walk."

"Let's do it."

The Nisga'a took the hint and reconvened with only four people on their side of the table.

Monday morning, in a team briefing, Doreen was exasperated. "It has cost upwards of seven hundred thousand dollars, this translation. When people write about this process—and they will write about it—this will come out."

That evening, the main table reconvened to approve the chapters that had been painstakingly translated and reviewed by Sylvain, a federal lawyer and me. We were in the thick of it, moving at a good pace, when a dashing young man in an expensive dark-blue suit burst into the room. When he realized that he was disrupting a large and intense meeting, he paused for a moment. Then, without missing a beat, he announced, "I need a phone. I have to call the prime minister. I told him I would report in once I had arrived."

Before he could say anything more, I guided him to a side room where there was a phone. He spoke to someone fervently in French, then turned to me and said, "I need privacy, please." What the hell would people think now with this dandy appearing on the scene, claiming to have a direct connection to the prime minister? It was late and none of my bosses were accessible. I would have to manage this man.

I waited outside until I heard silence, then opened the door and stepped in. I shook his hand as he introduced himself.

"This is amazing news, that Monsieur Chrétien has taken a personal interest in the process," I said to him in French. "Do you have a business card?"

Below the man's name was his title: *Advisor—Lands and Trusts—INAC, Hull, Quebec.*

"*Bon ben*, I don't work for him directly. We are friends. *Des amis particuliers.*"

"Well, that's great. I'm assigning you to the group working on the forestry chapter. You can head over now and get started."

"I'm tired, and I'm meeting friends for breakfast. I need to go back to my hotel to settle in."

"We need you to start now. We quit around ten o'clock and start back at eight in the morning. *Merci d'être venu.*"

A week later, thirty federal officials dined at a beautiful restaurant along False Creek, toasting one another as we admired the shimmering reflection of the lights of the Vancouver skyline on the ocean and exchanged tales of the craziness we had survived, the characters we'd dealt with. The food was sumptuous, and I wanted to savour it along with the others, enjoy my favourite red wine, but I couldn't relax. I wanted to go home.

I missed my little house overlooking the Salish Sea and the friends I had neglected for the past two months; increasingly, they were replacing my unpredictable family in my day-to-day life. I longed to renew my bond with my piano and guitar, to resume my morning smudge ceremonies and my meanderings along the stone-covered beach near my house. The next day, we were scheduled to have a brief ceremony with the Nisga'a leaders. Finally, I would get to meet Joseph Gosnell and shake his hand. It was as if I were going to meet the Dalai Lama, Liliuokalani, the last queen of Hawaii, or my Cree hero, Big Bear.

From the moment he entered the room, Chief Gosnell's poised stride, boisterous deep laugh and timeless gaze seemed to encapsulate the power and might of his ancestors. I so wanted to capture some of his energy and be blessed. When Doreen introduced us before the photo shoot, simply saying, "Darrel, this is Joe," I didn't know how to respond. I thought of him as Sim'oogit Hleekjust, even though I didn't know how to pronounce it. I blurted out something about being Cree from Treaty 8 territory. He took my hand in his and in a coarse baritone thanked me for my hard work.

I strolled down to Coal Harbour afterward to catch a float plane to Victoria. There was an aching hollow in my chest where I had pinned the souvenir brooch from the Nisga'a Final Agreement to my jacket: a medley of the flags of the Nisga'a, Canada and BC.

None of my friends or family would understand how I'd spent the last three months of my life, and I didn't know if I'd bother trying to explain it to them.

I was still melancholic a week later, as I sat on a stool in the Vancouver studio of the Canadian Broadcasting Corporation. This was my moment in the limelight: a French interview on national television about the Nisga'a Treaty, and there would be a fat overtime cheque coming soon. To help me focus, I reviewed a few terms from the French lexicon Sylvain and I had developed for the teams of translators to use:

Terres Nisga'a
Titre ancestral
Revenu de source propre
Restes humains

Canada Is Sorry

I BASKED IN THE thunderous drumming and booming chants of dozens of deep male voices, accompanied by the spectacle of women swaying rhythmically, woven cedar headbands over voluminous black hair, hands cupped and extended outwards, sketching waves in the air. This, followed by the boisterous introduction of their leaders in the Nuu-chah-nulth language, opened every session. Canada and BC were negotiating a modern treaty and land claim with the Nuu-chah-nulth people, who live on the west coast of Vancouver Island. It was the late nineties, and I couldn't believe I had been confirmed as senior negotiator for the Federal Treaty Office after over a year of acting in the position. I'd gone through a gruelling selection process—a written exam and interview—cutthroat competition against eighty other candidates.

"*Ha-wilth* is what we call a traditional chief. *Ha-wiah* is the plural," Cliff Atleo, a traditional chief from Ahousaht, proclaimed. I knew this, and I knew what came next. *Hahoolthe* meant the property of those chiefs: the land and all contained within it, including any captive enemies held as slaves. After that would come lengthy emphatic speeches in Nuu-chah-nulth. I didn't speak the language, so I had plenty of time to reflect on how I had come to know the meaning of *Ha-wilth* and *Hahoolthe* long before participating in these meetings.

A decade earlier, in the dreary rainy days of a Vancouver winter, in my warm classroom on the west side of the city, I had taught a social studies unit on Nuu-chah-nulth history and culture to my Grade Four class. We followed the readings, mini-lectures, discussions and films with an art project: ovoid and *U* shapes in red, white and black. (Years later, I would learn that the unit left out important information, like the fact that through the transmission of microbes, Europeans killed 90 per cent of the Nuu-chah-nulth people; that in the early 1800s two of their tribes took possession of two trading vessels, the *Boston* and the *Tonquin*; and the Nuu-chah-nulth history of cannibalism.)

Without ever meeting them, I had admired these dark stocky people of the fern-laden rainforest and misty coast. The men were valiant whale hunters and ruthless warriors with a propensity for beheading; skilled carvers and painters, storytellers. Women were talented weavers, traditional chiefs, gatherers and graceful dancers. A person of either gender could be a shaman. I knew I was romanticizing Nuu-chah-nulth life and culture to my students, but I couldn't help it. These people fascinated me. Now I wondered if I had somehow psychically ingratiated myself with them. Is that why I had ended up working with the Nuu-chah-nulth?

The opening scenario repeated itself at every meeting in one or the other of two large halls that up until the mid-1970s had been the gymnasiums of Alberni School, above the Somass River, and Christie School, on Tla-o-qui-aht lands above the beach near Clayoquot Sound. I always sat next to Paula, the cheery, intelligent young Italian Canadian who was our claims analyst. Paula kept her laptop and a bottle of water in front of her and the black barrister's bag holding our mandate documents and other records on the floor beside her. I came to think of her as the federal team's secret weapon. As I told friends, she was also my saviour, the only reason I survived the incredible stress of the job. The three representatives from the provincial government usually sat to the right of the federal team, which typically consisted of Chief Federal Negotiator Eric Denhoff, Paula and me. The Nuu-chah-nulth team of ten, which at the beginning had numbered into the thirties, usually sat across from us along a hollow octagon of tables. At coffee and lunch breaks, when the Nuu-chah-nulth weren't present, the provincial team would urge us, "Let's just get on with it—negotiate land and resource ownership and juris-diction, for god's sake," knowing we would not be able to provide any meaningful concessions to the Nuu-chah-nulth relating to the horrible legacy of residential schools. When they learned that Ron Irwin, the minister of Indian Affairs, under pressure from the Nuu-chah-nulth Tribal Council, had ordered the inclusion of residential schools as a topic for "substantive" negotiation, the provincial team couldn't resist gloating, guessing the federal team was in for a pounding given how emotionally charged the subject was.

"Residential schools were federally funded and operated. The provincial government had nothing to do with them and will not participate in discussions relating to this topic," the lawyer serving as the chief negotiator for BC asserted, and the Nuu-chah-nulth agreed, clearing the way for the creation of a bilateral working group that would meet twice a month to begin with, and then weekly. The chief federal negotiator designated me the federal lead on the subject, and I was relieved there would be no provincial representative present to obstruct what would be a challenging, if not futile, task.

M, the associate executive director of the Federal Treaty Office, was cynical and acerbic regarding residential schools as a matter for substantive negotiations. "What is your exit strategy, Darrel? We have no mandate to discuss residential schools or make any concessions on this topic. You will be wasting time and resources and creating expectations," he lectured.

"I understand. I will be very clear with the Nuu-chah-nulth that we have no mandate to discuss compensation or any such thing, but the issue made it into the framework agreement, so we have to hear them out."

"You'd better check in with PCO officials every step of the way. They'll be watching."

M, second-in-command at the treaty office, hadn't been present at my job interview or at the meeting where I was offered the position and had warned my future boss, Lynne Gregor, "I am a social activist and will be working for change. If that isn't acceptable, please don't hire me." Now he had created a no-win scenario for me and my team. The Privy Council Office, the secretariat to the Federal Cabinet that managed the residential school file, was inaccessible to someone at my level; nobody there would return my calls. And we all knew the thinking of the Department of Justice: a federal apology was paramount to admitting guilt and liability, so we couldn't go there.

I stacked this challenge on top of all the others. The criticism and anger came from all fronts. During my first negotiation session at the tripartite table, the chief of Tla-o-qui-aht First Nation had ridiculed me, asking me what I was doing on the federal side of the table. Feeling cheeky I answered, "Don't you think they need some help?" A Cree friend, a spiritual man and former chief, accused me of being a sellout, and an Indigenous academic I had been instrumental in hiring at the University of Victoria when I'd been special advisor in BC Advanced Education had said publicly that an Indigenous person working for change from within was anathema and had had me removed from UVic's external advisory committee. As a federal negotiator, the provincial government thought I was too sympathetic to First Nations and staged regular ambushes for me, the most dramatic of which was a vehement demand by a chief negotiator for BC that I disclose the federal mandate on whale hunting at an open main table session, and he'd had reporters waiting outside to interview me on the subject. Luckily the Nuu-chah-nulth rallied to the cause and blasted him for unprofessional behaviour that could have derailed the entire process. A fellow federal negotiator publicly accused me of leaking our mandate to a BC First Nation. My direct boss worried about a conflict of interest on my part as an Aboriginal, even though I was Cree from Alberta. And Eric, the chief federal negotiator, had also designated me to lead another problematic file: fisheries. But I knew I was supposed to be at that table, and I was so driven that I was almost impervious to the conflicts. I wasn't sure where my confidence and motivation were coming from then, but I was in fine form—clear-headed, alert, confident, perhaps even aloof. It may have been my newfound spiritual practices—the sense that I was in touch with and accompanied by my ancestors—or the validation and love of the group of friends I had established in Vancouver and Victoria. Or maybe I was simply doing what I was destined to do.

❖

I certainly wasn't impervious to what we heard at our working group on residential schools. One lovely brown face after another screwed up in sorrow and anger as people recounted trauma at residential school. The worst story we heard was that of children having needles stuck into their tongues for speaking Nuu-chah-nulth, which everyone called "Indian" at the time, just as they did Cree, Anishnabe and Haida. I thought of the story Mother had told me about her and Auntie Margaret being forced to go barefoot and survive on bread and water for two days as punishment for speaking Cree at St. Bernard's Indian Residential School at Buffalo Bay. Needles in the tongue was wicked beyond belief. I wanted to scream, weep and yell at the terrible injustice. Instead, I listened intently, jotting down notes.

There must have been ghosts at our meetings in those two former gymnasiums. I didn't sense or see them, but the meetings were always fraught with problems—technical difficulties, direct personal attacks, hyped-up drama and vitriol. In spite of the horrific history of student abuse and even deaths, I felt at ease and empowered being in Nuu-chah-nulth territory, on their lands, in their company. Did the spirits of former students and their ancestors help me to get through the discussions?

"How can you sit there impassively and listen to this in your comfortable government job? You can go to your fancy hotel room afterwards and forget about all of this, while we suffer," a Nuu-chah-nulth negotiator shouted at me one afternoon. "We live with the consequences of this legacy of torture and terror." I was thankful that I had prayed to the spirits of the place and meditated for a few moments before entering the hall.

"There aren't enough hours in a day, days in a month, months in a year to hear all of your legitimate grievances," I replied. "The experience was horrendous, and I wish there was something tangible I could offer you at this point, but there isn't. We have been clear about this from the beginning. Knowing this, can you tell us what it is you hope we can do?"

George Watts, a powerful chief whose traditional name was Wameesh, spoke up: "An apology. A sincere and heartfelt apology from the federal government to the Nuu-chah-nulth. We have a process for helping survivors to advance their individual cases through the courts, and we will continue that work. But at this table, we want to negotiate a residential school apology."

"Thank you for your clarity. My instructions haven't changed, but I will discuss this with senior officials, and we'll give you an answer during our next main table session in a few weeks."

❖

The next week, Eric Denhoff and I travelled to Ottawa to meet with officials from the Privy Council Office and the Department of Justice to clarify whether to continue discussions about an apology or to make a final statement that there was nothing we could do on this issue. The Nuu-chah-nulth had been clear—there would be no final agreement without some movement on the residential school file. Were they bluffing? Eric and I met our DOJ and PCO colleagues in the ominous complex called les Terrasses de la Chaudière on the Hull side of the Ottawa River.

Shawn Tupper from PCO spoke first. "We can't discuss compensation. We can discuss a monument to acknowledge the legacy of residential schools. That, possibly with some sort of carefully worded statement that does not admit culpability. The concern, of course, is liability—there are over a hundred thousand living survivors, and if each of them were to receive compensation, we could be talking a billion and a half dollars." DOJ lawyer Mitch Taylor nodded in agreement.

"A fruitless fucking meeting," Eric muttered through gritted teeth in the elevator down.

"We've got our foot in the door, Eric. This has legs."

"Yeah, good luck. You know the associate ED of the treaty office hates this file."

❖

Our next meeting with the Nuu-chah-nulth didn't go well.

"A monument? A memorial? A collective gravestone for all the children who didn't come back—who died at the schools? This is an insult!" George Watts bellowed as he threw the *Vancouver Sun* onto the table in front of him. "We need and demand an apology. I will be calling the minister—be forewarned."

The next day was policy caucus in Vancouver. I hated those meetings. Twenty or so senior federal officials, each trying to outsmart the rest. One radically fascist, another very liberal, and at the next session they would switch roles. As the only Indigenous person in the room, and one of only two people who weren't white, I was often in the difficult position of having to decide whether to speak up or to stay mum and swallow the blatant bigotry of what I heard.

Two of the topics on the lengthy agenda were related to my files: fisheries enforcement and a residential school apology for the Nuu-chah-nulth. The enforcement discussion went badly. "Picture it—Indians with guns threatening white guys," bellowed one chief negotiator—abhorring the idea of Indigenous people becoming full-fledged armed fisheries officers. I couldn't resist responding. "Well, I have a cousin—a Cree cousin—who is an RCMP inspector. He can arrest and detain *anyone* who breaks the law, at gunpoint if necessary. Times have changed, my friend."

After an awkward silence, the chair quickly shifted the discussion to the apology question. It was predictably exasperating.

"An apology on residential schools would set a precedent. All of the groups negotiating will demand the same. It will be a tremendous distraction. And we have no mandate for this," said a Japanese Canadian senior negotiator who I had thought would be sympathetic.

"The Nuu-chah-nulth Tribal Council is the only group who have demanded this be listed as a matter to be negotiated in their framework agreement," I countered.

"The deputy minister hates the concept. We will not do an apology," declared M, the Federal Treaty Office's associate ED.

"Well, let's not be so sure," the executive director chimed in, causing all present to look confused. Usually she and the associate ED were on the same page.

Eric seized the opportunity. "Privy Council and the Department of Justice are open to it, and there is no other concession we can make at this table on the topic."

I knew M wasn't convinced, but he couldn't contradict

both his boss and a chief federal negotiator with strong political connections. Instead, after the meeting, he cornered me. "Listen, you know the deputy minister hates this. Make it go away."

Pursuing the apology was the right thing to do. I was convinced of that. But I knew there would be a price to pay. I desperately wanted to discuss my dilemma with my close friends but I couldn't. I was sworn to secrecy.

❖

A few days after the policy caucus meeting, I enjoyed a brief early-morning respite, walking along Nanaimo Harbour in the sunshine with chirping songbirds all around and float planes bouncing over gentle whitecaps as they landed. As usual I picked up a newspaper to read over breakfast. The Blackwater Alberni Residential School case was making headlines.

It was a short stroll to the Coast Bastion Hotel where we would meet with the Nuu-chah-nulth and BC. Paula was gone by now—she had taken a leave to study dance. The large meeting room was set up in a hollow square with white modesty panels hanging from the tables and lighting as bright as an interrogation room. The chandeliers sparkled mercilessly. I sensed the tension as soon as I walked into the room. George Watts's classic white dress shirt already had damp patches around the armpits—not a good sign. Stern faces filled the room. I ducked into a chair beside Dan, our new claims analyst.

To my surprise, the opening comment was directed at me. "I saw you and the BC negotiator walking hand in hand down the street last night," a Nuu-chah-nulth negotiator poked. "Makes sense, provincial and federal government in bed together, especially when going against the Indians. Who goes on top, or do you alternate?"

I let out a fake chuckle. The speaker must have known he was hitting a vulnerable spot. I was very private about my love life, to the extent that I had one. "The day a provincial negotiator holds my hand, I want a photo."

"Let's cut the nonsense and get started," the chairperson ordered. "Darrel, we have a pressing issue with the federal government. Outrageous fucking behaviour, just when we were beginning to trust you."

I inched my chair even closer to the table. The chairperson never swore. What in hell...?

The chiefs leaned back, arms crossed, and stared at the floor as the chair continued. "I was called by a private detective last week. He's gathering intel on residential school survivors. I know this isn't on the agenda today, but it doesn't matter. The chiefs won't discuss anything else until this matter is sorted out."

My face felt completely devoid of blood. Without Paula there to calm me and scribble me a note, I had to get my bearings on my own—grasp the issue and respond. The accusation was absurd, but the chairperson continued without giving me a chance to say anything.

"The detective was hired by the federal Department of Justice. He called and visited several former students, but he began with me, thinking that as the last principal of Alberni School, I would happily be an informant in exchange for money. Spill the beans on former students, those in the Blackwater court case and others. Wanted me to say they were making it all up—the physical and sexual abuse. He tried to get dirt on some of them: were they addicts, perverts, abusers? Had they been harmed in their own homes as toddlers and during summer vacations, rather than at school? Could *they* have victimized the school staff? He took for granted I would be complicit because I'm *Mamatli*—white. Darrel, you guys talk endlessly about a new relationship between the federal government and First Nations, about correcting past wrongs. How fucking hypocritical can one be?"

"Mr. Chair, there is no private eye," I said, shaken. "I don't know what you are talking about. We've been working with DOJ on this matter. They wouldn't do an end run around us—no way."

"I'm calling a break," said the chairperson, "and when we reconvene in an hour, you had better have some answers or we're calling the media."

I found a side room and called Shawn Tupper at the Privy Council Office. Through some miracle, I got him. He promised to check into the private eye issue and get back to me. I walked back to the harbour. The wind had picked up, and it was cold. The small whitecaps were now swells that broke like waves. Seagulls screeched and called from their perch atop tarred black telephone poles.

When the bulky cell in my briefcase vibrated, I fumbled to answer it.

A trembling voice. "Darrel—bad news. Turns out there is a private eye, and yes, he is on contract to DOJ. The team working on the Blackwater case hired him. They panicked, sure they were going to lose. They needed intelligence on the plaintiffs—sexual history, criminal behaviour and so on."

It was a disaster. There was no question, now the Nuu-chah-nulth would reject the looming comprehensive land and cash offer that had been years in the making. I felt so betrayed. It turned out I was working for the dark side after all. I went right down to the water to collect my thoughts and plan a strategy.

I had no choice but to return to the hotel. Humiliated, livid and fighting back tears, I apologized profusely on behalf of the federal government and asked that the meeting be adjourned.

❖

A week later, I was in my office reviewing a memorandum to cabinet regarding another file when I got a surprise phone call from lawyer Mitch Taylor: "There's been a change of heart in DOJ, Darrel. It has been decided that an apology doesn't necessarily increase liability. In fact, it may go some way toward deflecting anger and decreasing the number of victims who will sue us. We might be able to do a limited apology after all."

I informed the Nuu-chah-nulth of the new thinking in DOJ, and within a week they had a text they said a federal apology would have to contain. The text—dramatic, detailed—would mean a blatant admission of culpability on the part of the federal government. I balked at this latest development, as did Eric and Dan. Nevertheless, I passed the text on to Mitch Taylor, warning him of its content. He said he would need time to get back to us— months, not weeks.

After Dan, Eric and I had endured many combative sessions with the Nuu-chah-nulth and the province, negotiating matters like the selection of treaty settlement lands, fish allocations, forestry, copyright, the repatriation of cultural artifacts and human remains, certainty and the relationship of laws, Mitch Taylor called to say he was ready to schedule a meeting with the Nuu-chah-nulth.

Given that it was a working group meeting rather than a main table session, we skipped the usual opening formalities and began instead with a brief prayer by an elder. Then we turned the meeting over to Mitch. He began in a quiet tone.

"I know we haven't met in a while; I apologize, but we needed time to analyze the text you proposed for an apology, and as you can imagine, this takes time. After intense deliberations in government at several levels, finally I have a text to discuss with you. It is extremely confidential, so there are no copies."

Was Mitch's voice becoming unsteady? What would he say next? He had told our team only that he thought the federal government's proposed text would go some way toward meeting the Nuu-chah-nulth demands. As usual, his dark eyes were bursting with intelligence and empathy. His thick facial hair likely hadn't been shaven for twenty-four hours, as if he had been stewing over his work all night. I had my back to a large bank of windows that looked into a dreary parking lot. Seagulls heckled in the background. In a few hours, Mitch would be on a plane back to Ottawa, but Dan and I would have to live with the consequences.

George Watts looked ready to explode as he waved a hand in the air. "Fine, read it out then. We gave you our text for an apology and you balked. You guys are afraid o' your own shadow, for Chris' sake. Just read it."

Mitch bowed his head, shuffled the papers in front of him and began.

> I am here today on behalf of the Government of Canada to apologize to the Nuu-chah-nulth people for Canada's role in the Indian residential school system that has profoundly affected your people for over one hundred years.
>
> Sadly, our history with respect to the treatment of Aboriginal people, including Nuu-chah-nulth, is not something in which we can take pride. Attitudes of racial and cultural superiority led to a suppression of Aboriginal culture and values. As a country, we are burdened by past actions that resulted in weakening the identity of Nuu-chah-nulth peoples, suppressing their languages and cultures and outlawing spiritual practices. We recognize the impact of these actions on the once self-sustaining nations that were disaggregated, disrupted, limited or even destroyed by the dispossession of traditional territory, by the relocation of Aboriginal peoples, including Nuu-chah-nulth, and by some provisions of the Indian Act. We acknowledge that the result of these actions was the erosion of the political, economic and

social systems of Aboriginal peoples and nations, including Nuu-chah-nulth.

Everyone was listening, but visibly getting restless. Was he going to continue the bureaucratic bafflegab and put us all to sleep? Was that the government's strategy?

> Over the past year, representatives of the Department of Indian Affairs and Northern Development (DIAND) have been meeting with representatives of your communities to talk about the impacts of the Indian residential school system and what needs to be done to address the legacy of this system and the ongoing issues you confront. One of the things we have learned is that Canada needs to acknowledge its role in the development and administration of this system and the impact this system has had on your lives. This apology to the Nuu-chah-nulth will serve as a basis for creating a new set of relationships between the Nuu-chah-nulth and the Government of Canada and to create hope for more respectful relationships in the future.

> As many of you know, Canada's first step in acknowledging its role in developing and administering the system of Indian residential schools was through the Statement of Reconciliation delivered by the former minister of DIAND on January 8, 1998.

George Watts crossed his arms and rested them on his protruding belly.

Since that statement was delivered, Canada's representatives have, at the invitation of your community, been meeting with the Nuu-chah-nulth in order to learn more about your community's experiences in Indian residential schools. We have learned that approximately 5,000 Nuu-chah-nulth attended eight Indian residential schools in British Columbia: Ahousaht Indian Residential School;
Alberni Indian Residential School;
Christie Indian Residential School;
Coqualeetza Indian Residential School;
Kamloops Indian Residential School;
Kuper Island Indian Residential School;
St. Mary's Indian Residential School and
St. Michael's Indian Residential School.

Canada shared in the administration and operation of these Indian residential schools with one of the Anglican, Catholic or United churches who oversaw their day-to-day running. Through their history, these schools separated Nuu-chah-nulth children from other children attending school in British Columbia. Nuu-chah-nulth languages and cultural practices were not respected in these schools. We have heard that while some former students have spoken positively about their experiences at residential schools, such stories are far overshadowed by tragic stories of abuse, separation from families, the impacts on Nuu-chah-nulth languages and culture and of a legacy which contributes to social problems which continue to exist in your communities today.

Complete silence. People glanced around, catching each other's gazes across the room, then looking away. Mitch kept his head down.

> And so it is the Nuu-chah-nulth experiences which bring us here today. Many Nuu-chah-nulth children did not escape this tragedy. Former Nuu-chah-nulth students have made disclosures of physical, sexual and emotional abuse and about losing their connection to their culture, language and families.

Mitch coughed and cleared his throat. Stillness reigned in the room.

> Sadly, some Nuu-chah-nulth former students have had to tell of their experiences in a courtroom. These are not easy stories to hear. We can only imagine how hard they are to tell, and how much harder yet they were to have lived. We are all humbled by the dignity and courage these individuals have shown in coming forward and sharing these experiences.

> Former students have talked about the loneliness which resulted from separation from families and that this separation led to the loss of relationships with their families. Many of the students returned to their communities unable to take up their responsibilities within their families or communities due to a loss of language and a loss of knowledge of traditional ceremonies.

> We will never hear the stories of those children who died in an Indian residential school and did not return home.

Mitch's voice cracked. Coughs around the room and several people reaching for their glasses of water. I took a deep breath and heard Dan do the same. Good god, was he really saying this?

> We have learned, both from the *Nitinaht Chronicles* and the Nuu-chah-nulth report on Indian residential schools how the legacy of residential schools has contributed to other social problems arising in former students, including addictions, unstable family relationships, poor health, anger, confusion and shame about their identities as Nuu-chah-nulth people. The Indian residential school system disrupted the transfer of appropriate parenting skills and introduced models of discipline which were not in your tradition.

It was so quiet you could have heard eagle down swirling and spiralling, as in the most sacred of dances. Were people even breathing?

> Canada apologizes to the Nuu-chah-nulth people for its role in planning, designing, building and administering the system of Indian residential schools and accepts that the existence of the schools was profoundly disrespectful of Aboriginal people.

> Canada apologizes for all the suffering of Nuu-chah-nulth children who were victims in these institutions of emotional, physical and sexual abuse.

> Canada apologizes to those Nuu-chah-nulth families whose children returned from Indian residential schools unable to take up their responsibilities

within their families due to loss of language and loss of knowledge of traditional ceremonies.

Canada apologizes to those individuals who have had to struggle alone where their lack of Nuu-chah-nulth language has prevented them from hearing the teachings of their parents and grandparents or understanding the traditional ceremonies and disrupted their spiritual, mental and emotional connection to the land and its resources.

Canada acknowledges the legacy that has been left by Indian residential schools and apologizes to those generations who have been affected and continue to be affected by this legacy.

Canada apologizes for the loneliness endured by those who were separated from their parents, siblings, elders and other family members through their attendance at Indian residential schools.

Canada apologizes for the emotional burden placed on mothers, fathers, sisters, brothers and grandparents who had members of their families attending Indian residential schools and the effect this separation had on the bonds within those families.

I looked around the room. Most people were dabbing their eyes. Was this for real? Had this text been approved? Surely the government couldn't put this out there and then take it away. I was terrified I was about to lose my composure and start blubbering.

> Canada apologizes and offers condolences to those
> Nuu-chah-nulth families whose children died and
> never returned home from Indian residential schools.

Now my tears flowed, and I didn't have to look up to know that everyone else was crying.

Just then the cellphone in our barrister's bag buzzed like an angry wasp trying to escape confinement. Dan handed it to me, and I ducked out of the room. It was Lynne, our boss: "The commercial fishers are demanding a bilateral meeting to discuss the approach we're taking on salmon allocations with the Nuu-chah-nulth. They've written to the minister."

❖

On the warm sunny afternoon of December 9, 2000, in the gymnasium of the former Alberni Indian Residential School in Port Alberni, DIAND Deputy Minister Shirley Serafini read the entire text of the apology. Afterward, I stepped outside and wandered down to the shore of the Somass River. What had just happened here? Would it make a difference?

The Supreme Court of Canada would conclude the appeal of the Blackwater case in October 2005. By that time, I would be working in Ottawa for the Assembly of First Nations. I had followed the case since it began in 1996. The decision at the trial level had been appealed to the Supreme Court of BC, and that court's judgment in turn was appealed by the federal government to the Supreme Court of Canada. The morning I spotted the *Globe and Mail* headlines saying the Supreme Court had issued its ruling on the case, I rushed back to my office to download the complete decision, which was final and executory.

Several paragraphs leapt off the page, burning their way into my mind and heart despite the legal bafflegab. Repeated again and again was a word I had learned through this case but wished I hadn't: *vicariously*. (The emphasis below is mine.)

> The Government of Canada and the United Church of Canada operated an Indian residential school in British Columbia in the 1940s, 1950s and 1960s. Aboriginal children were taken from their families pursuant to the Indian Act and sent to the school. They were disciplined by corporal punishment. Some, like the appellant B, were repeatedly and brutally sexually assaulted. Four actions were commenced in 1996 by former residents of the school claiming damages for sexual abuse and other harm. The trial judge found that all claims other than those of a sexual nature were statute-barred. P, a dormitory supervisor, was held liable for sexual assault. Canada was held liable for the assaults on the basis of breach of nondelegable statutory duty, and also because Canada and the Church were jointly and *vicariously* liable for these wrongs. Fault was apportioned 75 per cent to Canada and 25 per cent to the Church. The trial judge awarded $125,000 general damages and $20,000 aggravated damages to B against the Church and Canada. A further $40,000 punitive damages, plus a future counselling fee of $5,000, was awarded to B against P. Other plaintiffs were awarded amounts commensurate with their situations. The Court of Appeal applied a doctrine of charitable immunity to exempt the Church from liability and placed all liability on Canada on the basis of *vicarious* liability, awarding B an additional $20,000 for loss of future earning opportunity. Otherwise, it maintained the differing awards for sexual abuse.

Held: B's appeal is dismissed (he had asked that the compensation award be increased). Canada's appeal is allowed in part. The judgment of the trial judge on the issues of joint *vicarious* liability against the Church and Canada, and assessment and apportionment of damages, is restored. The judgment of the Court of Appeal on the issue of charitable immunity is set aside. The Court of Appeal's award for loss of future earning opportunity is upheld.

The Church exerted sufficient control over the operations at the residential school that gave rise to the wrong to be found *vicariously liable with Canada* for the wrongful acts of P. The trial judge's factual findings clearly support a conclusion that the Church was one of P's employers in every sense of the word.

None of the considerations relied on by the Court of Appeal—Canada's degree of control over the residential school, the Church's specific mandate of promoting Christian education and the difficulty of holding two defendants *vicariously* liable for the same wrong—negate the imposition of *vicarious liability* on the Church.

Similarly, the Court of Appeal erred in exempting the Church from liability on the ground of charitable immunity. A class-based exemption from *vicarious* liability finds support neither in principle nor in the jurisprudence. Exempting nonprofit organizations when government is present would not motivate such organizations to take precautions to screen their employees and protect children from sexual abuse. *The presence of the government does not guarantee the safety of children*, particularly where, as in this case, the nonprofit organization has day-to-day management of the institution.

I was happy that after almost twenty years there was some level of closure for the plaintiffs—the survivors—even though the compensation amounts seemed low, especially given that the Supreme Court ruled that each party should bear its own costs. That meant the survivors' legal fees would come out of their awards, which were already much less than those in the Mount Cashel Orphanage case.

I was distressed when I came to the section of the decision where names of legal counsel for the various parties were listed and I saw who had been the DOJ lead for the federal government: "Mitchell R. Taylor and James M. Ward, for the appellant/respondent Her Majesty the Queen in Right of Canada, as represented by the Minister of Indian Affairs and Northern Development."

The trial had been underway at the same time we were negotiating the apology with the Nuu-chah-nulth. There may not have been a legal requirement for DOJ's lawyer to disclose that he was working all sides of the issue, but I couldn't help but think the Nuu-chah-nulth should have been informed.

An even more troubling thought relating to my role in the apology to the Nuu-chah-nulth entered my mind as I trudged back to my sparsely furnished Ottawa apartment. Had the Supreme Court of Canada been more lenient toward the federal government because of their seemingly authentic apology to the Nuu-chah-nulth? Had I been instrumental in victimizing survivors of the Alberni residential school yet again: *vicariously*?

The Carved Cedar Bentwood Box
in the Trunk

HAD I ALWAYS wanted to be white, or was it simply a desire
to be cool, cocky and confident like the white kids I grew
up with, so sure of themselves? I might also be happier if
I were Asian, I thought. At least then I'd have a clear identity and
be able to live, work and play in my birth language in many cities
of the world. From the time I was a small boy, people had accused
me of being Chinese. "Are you Perry Mah's twin brother?" kids
would goad before launching into a lilting chorus of *chinky chinky
chinaman, sitting on a fence, tryna make a dollar outta fifteen
cents.*

Strange thoughts to be having as I opened the trunk of my
car to quickly inspect the urns I had wrapped in a red and black
button blanket and placed gently into the carved cedar bentwood
box, yearning to go up to the cafeteria level of the boat for my first
coffee of the day.

A blond Rasta man sauntered up the rocking, sun-filled ramp
of the 11:00 a.m. ferry from Swartz Bay to Tsawwassen. A swelling

crowd of Chinese nationals in steel-blue uniforms with black crew-cuts pushed past, chatting amongst themselves while swivelling their heads from side to side to glimpse screaming seagulls. The blond man's blend of sandalwood and pot as he brushed by took me back to my high school days: Western Canada High, Calgary, mid-seventies. Every lunch break I would stand on the front steps of the sprawling red brick building, my stomach grumbling, to watch the scrum of guys huddled off to one side, toking up. Their devil-may-care attitude made me feel like a nervous laboratory rat. How uptight, ordinary and dull I must have seemed. The aroma of burned French roast from the tall paper cup the Rasta man held in his unwashed, perfect hand and the slight to and fro movement of the huge boat brought me back to the present. *Salt Spring Roasting Company*, the label read—the brand I drank when I first moved to Victoria. I loved their Mocha Java, but Trina and Milan had found it weak.

The white Rasta man sat on the floor near the video arcade on deck five, got out his guitar, set its tattered black case in front of him and began to tune. Nearly identical front-page photos from the *Vancouver Sun*, the *Globe and Mail* and usa *Today* in the hands of passengers seated around us formed a fractured mural: the twin towers—a coal-black cumulus cloud blasting out of one, a golden fireball out of the other. *Teewaaanguh teewaaanguh.* The sound repeated in rapid succession, from bass to high notes, as the ship's horn blasted a long deep moan. People continued to mill past, and I wondered if the man was going to busk. What was it about him that intrigued me—the fact he played music, probably reggae, or was it the beehive of dark golden hair that wafted up off his head and then cascaded into shredded wheat dreadlocks?

Concert B flat, that's what trumpet players tuned to. The violins to something else, as I recalled, A at the top of a D minor triad, and the French horns and trombones to something different altogether, probably F—F major. *A Sea Symphony* by Vaughan Williams—that was the first symphonic piece I'd ever heard, and my friend Anne Butterworth, who was in her first year of university then, sang the soprano solo. I was awestruck by the rich tone of her voice, its consistent flow and subtle tremolo. Anne wore a plain white blouse and a pleated black skirt the day of the final concert at the Jubilee Auditorium in Edmonton. This was similar to what she usually wore; she dressed sensibly, like a nun. I was in a puffy yellow dress shirt and jeans. What would Anne think now of this Rasta man, his look, his smell, his unkempt flaxen beard, paisley kaftan shirt, tan-coloured jeans and matching workboots? His bottomless cobalt-blue eyes? I could just hear her: what a waste of talent, trying to be something he's not, throwing away his own culture and heritage trying to be Jamaican; he obviously comes from a privileged background; he should be studying something. And what would she have thought back then about Trina, who at the time was in the early stages of her transgender metamorphosis? I never did tell Anne about her. Anne's family owned a Tudor-style house on the south side of Edmonton, overlooking the North Saskatchewan River, and she was already a respected musician and academic. Surely she would have had to reject me if she'd found out I had a transgender sibling.

The only person who would kiss me during the music camp where I met Anne was a very overweight girl with long chestnut-brown hair (Anne may have kissed me, but it took time for me to realize that she liked me). Nobody had asked the girl to dance at the sock hop after the variety show where she had sat frozen at a table onstage while another pair of hands, those of a guy concealed behind her, applied her makeup—powdered her eyebrows and drew cherry lips on her forehead, encouraged by guffaws from the teenaged crowd. Sitting in the tall grass of the campus fields, we got through one awkward kiss before we both realized we were hiding.

Trina had been fat too (her words), and she thought this helped her pass as a cisgender woman. I was chubby as an early teen but went on a crash diet—yoghurt and nuts for two weeks—to lose my spare tire. So I was slim by the summer after Grade Eleven, but I still wasn't attractive (though years later I would understand it had little to do with my looks or weight).

❖

The rasta man must have sensed I was studying him (the fresh blemish on his nose, specks of dirt under his uncut finger-nails) and conjuring his soulmate, a fair Rasta girl whose neck he nuzzled with his puffy pink lips and fuzzy facial hair. He fastened a capo around the neck of his guitar, then tucked its curvy body into his lap and reached for his pick. I hoped he would look over, compelled by my penetrating gaze. Would it offend or trouble him? Would he pity me if I told him I was about to drive a couple thousand kilometres to a tiny village in northern Alberta to bury Trina, my transgender sister? Would he sense how distraught and afraid I was to do this alone and offer to come along for the ride, perhaps even drive a stretch of the journey that would take us up the Coquihalla Highway, through the desert of Kamloops, along the Thompson River and then through the snow-capped Rocky Mountains of Jasper National Park?

Maybe that was how Trina's one ride in my black BMW sports car—the ride I had promised her once she got over her outrage that I had bought a Bimmer instead of giving her a down payment on a condo—would turn out, me with my hair tied back into a wavy salt-and-pepper ponytail, flying at 160 kilometres an hour along the eight-lane freeway with the sunroof open, a ripe wannabe Rasta man sprawled in the passenger seat, while Trina and her favourite cat, Cleopatra, rode in urns inside the carved cedar bentwood box in the trunk.

It had all begun one sunny Friday afternoon. I had just completed three days of transition meetings in Vancouver, leading the closure of the Victoria treaty office and laying off twenty talented negotiators and analysts, including friends, because M, who had been promoted to executive director, wanted to "reel us in." Lynne and I had made grown men and women cry.

As I was leaving the Pacific Palisades Hotel, crows dive-bombed me. I dropped my briefcase and ducked under a sculpted Japanese maple, chills up to my neck. Oh my god, it was happening again. As Mother had always warned, the crows carried a message, and I got it: somebody was going to die. I choked back tears and begged the universe—please, oh please, not now. I stood there for a moment. Should I go to see Trina right away, spend one more night in Vancouver? I glanced over the lush manicured lawn and sculpted evergreens, then at Grouse Mountain in the distance.

Surely Trina would hang on. I had just helped her settle at home after a long stay in the hospital, and she was improving. Tomorrow I would order her Meals on Wheels. I needed the solace and quiet of my little house in the forest on Vancouver Island—it had been a tough week. I darted and weaved my way through the first wave of rush-hour traffic, drove onto the Victoria ferry and hurried up to the outer deck to relax. The crows were just being crows—they did that to a lot of people, especially people with black hair. Instead of burying my head in briefing books, I sat cross-legged atop the bin of life preservers, hoping to see bald eagles circling above as the boat swayed and shuddered through Active Pass. The eagles would give me strength and clarity—confirm that everything was okay. But there were none.

Exhilaration on seeing the Olympic Mountains across the strait and tasting the fresh cool island air rushing in through the sunroof. During the thirty-kilometre drive from Saanich to Sooke, the external temperature dropped from twenty-six degrees to twenty. I pictured what I would do when I arrived home—rush to my garden to see what was ready; run five kilometres along the beach; savour miso soup, probably with fresh snow peas and purple broccoli; and perch myself by the fire with a glass of red wine and a hand-rolled Drum cigarette. Then the best part— stretch out on the couch to finish reading *La saga des Béothuks*, a tragic but fascinating story about the extinction of an entire tribe in Newfoundland.

These thoughts calmed me, and I was starting to unwind when three brief screams of a siren pulled me out of my daydream. Shit, where did that cop car come from? Suddenly it was right behind me with its red and blue lights flashing in the rear-view mirror. Cops were never out here, but yes, going through town you had to be careful not to go even a few kilometres over the limit. Damn, I couldn't have been going *that* fast.

The cop stepped out of his car and slowly approached with his hand on the holster of his revolver. Why did they always do that? A bare giant maple stood across the road. Most of its crimson and orange leaves covered the ground, but some still swirled in the wind on low branches.

"Where you goin' in such a rush?"

"West."

"Where are you coming from?"

"East."

"Oh, it's going to be like that, is it? Let's see your stuff," the cop said, pointing toward my glove compartment.

I handed him the papers and gripped the steering wheel tightly with both hands.

"You live out on West Coast Road? You're Darrel McLeod? Well, what a coincidence. I was just on my way out to see you. Your sister is dead."

"What are you talking about? I just spoke to her. She's fine," I bluffed, hoping he would realize he was mistaken and apologize for being so crass.

"Trina Lee McLeod—she was found dead yesterday afternoon in a Native housing project, Downtown Eastside of Vancouver.

"Oh my god." I crumpled into a ball and fell toward the passenger side.

"Uh, sorry... I didn't know how else to tell you. You're free to go."

❖

The rasta man was singing Bob Marley's "One Love" to a convincing reggae rhythm on the guitar. How could I find the courage to ask him to join me? Or should I try to find David, my shirt-tail cousin from Sturgeon Lake First Nation and sometime lover, to make the trip north with me? David knew my family situation and understood our culture. As a droning voice announced that we were nearing Tsawwassen, I watched the Rasta man pack up and sling his backpack and guitar over his shoulder. Maybe we would meet again—perhaps on the ferry ride home in a week or so. I held on to this hope as I impatiently inched the car toward the off-ramp, then accelerated onto the expressway to speed through the depths of the George Massey Tunnel and along the freeway to Vancouver. I wondered where I would find David and if he would be clean.

Late that afternoon I picked up Milan and Trina's best friend, Donnie, to accompany me to the funeral home. Donnie had worked as a trans server for thirty years and I had always wondered if he really liked Trina or simply pitied her. I soon regretted bringing Milan and Donnie, because what came next was horrific.

The tall, acne-faced undertaker rolled out a narrow trolley with a huge black plastic garbage bag flopping over its sides. He gave me a smile, then abruptly reached into the bag's centre with large scissors and snipped it. A flaccid arm fell down, and a putrid odour slammed us. Milan gagged and fled, but Donnie managed to touch Trina's hand and say, "Goodbye, dear Trina. You were a good friend," before gliding away. That left me—and I couldn't leave. I had to see her face and stay with her a while to say my farewells. I slid a metal folding chair closer to the trolley and swallowed back the acidic liquid percolating in my throat. I began to reminisce: the time Greggie pulled me out of the Athabasca River when I was five and had run into the water after a fish that got away. How when I was seven and he thirteen we braved the harrowing howls of coyotes and wolves to traipse into the dark, snowy forest in search of the perfect Christmas tree because our stepfather was drinking and Mother was desperate. I pictured Trina working as a waitress at the Aristocratic on Granville and Broadway, so beautiful in her starched uniform with her hair tucked under her peaked cap. Her beaming face when she graduated from the nursing program at Vancouver Community College.

She had suffered trying to be something she couldn't be. She told me that after having worked for years with female nurses who didn't have a clue she was trans, not even the few who had become close friends—she realized she would always feel like an imposter, inventing stories about heavy periods, wild orgasms, mammograms and birth control. A week before she died, she had set up a dinner for the two of us at the Old Spaghetti Factory in Gastown so she could apologize for all the horrible things she had ever said and done to me. I thanked her but was confounded. Had she really taken stock of all of the abuse and animosity she'd levelled at me over the years? Even if she had, did she expect it all to dissipate with a simple apology?

There beside the trolley, I wiped my face with the back of my hand and stood to leave.

❖

Early the next day, I picked up David in front of the funeral home and crematorium. A McDonald's drive-through for breakfast, and then we headed onto the Trans-Canada. We were on the flat stretch through the Fraser Valley when the shrill ring of my cellphone startled us. A nasal voice on speakerphone.

"Hello, Darrel McLeod? It's Joan Lyons, your sister Trina's addictions doctor. You must have known she was on the methadone program the last few years of her life."

"Yes, Dr. Lyons. Trina really admired you."

"I just wanted to tell you, Trina mentioned you in every appointment. She said you were so caring, very kind to her, always."

A rush of tears. I pulled over and mumbled a thank you. I flicked the windshield wipers on and then quickly off. Feeling stupid, I glanced at David's angular, morose Cree face framed by long black hair. He cared, but maybe I should have asked the white Rasta man along after all. He would have distracted me in powerful ways and kept me from getting sucked into the vortex of my despair. With David around I had to stay in control, be vigilant.

The rest of the journey was a blur. I uttered a prayer to our ancestors at Mount Robson and noticed a new continental divide marker as we entered Alberta. How symbolic—we might as well have been crossing a force field to enter another universe.

The next day in Edmonton, alone, I drove Jasper Avenue, the strip where Trina used to hustle as a teenaged drag queen. I passed the small store that had been Dolly Donut, the place where all the queens hung out late at night and met for coffee early the next afternoon. Concentrate, I reminded myself. Flowers... you have to buy a couple of wreaths before heading to Smith. A spray of long-stemmed roses, she loved red roses, and food for the reception afterwards, Ritz crackers, cheddar cheese, dill pickles and kolbassa. I couldn't expect Auntie Rosie and Uncle Charlie to provide everything. They had looked after all the other funerals, and what did they owe us? We had left Smith in 1967, when I was nine and Trina fifteen. She had never returned.

I bought the *Edmonton Sun* and flipped past the photo of the busty blonde Sunshine Girl to find the obituary I paid to run for a week. That would cause a stir. In it I had attempted to sound at once poetic and spiritual:

> At the age of 48, Greg/Trina McLeod, our dear brother/sister, has gone to the other side. S/he trained and worked as a nurse and was an animal rights and smoking activist. Greg/Trina will join those who have gone before us to prepare the way: our loving Father and Mother, Sonny and Bertha, our oldest sister, Debbie, younger brother, Travis and stepfather, Edward.

❖

I sighed as I pulled into the muddy driveway in front of Auntie Rosie's house. She was the matriarch of what remained of our waning clan. She had always guarded Trina and my Aunt Diane— from their early childhood years into adulthood.

Everyone cherished Auntie Rosie's timid chuckle, and on the evening Father Giguère came to her house to bless Trina's remains, it was infectious.

"Why *two h*'urns?" the octogenarian priest asked, his trembling hand suspended mid-air three-quarters of the way through the sign of the cross. The two grey onyx urns were nestled into the black and red button blanket in the cedar bentwood box.

A worried look crossed Auntie's face—I had to speak up.

"The smaller one is her cat," I explained. "She adored that *minoos*, and she asked in her will that I collect the urn with the cat's ashes from its shrine in her home and bury it with her."

"*Bon dieu*, but cats—*les chats*, they don't '*ave h'a* soul." The priest frowned, and his hand dropped. Looking perplexed, he glared at Auntie, then me.

For a second we stared back at him, speechless. Then Auntie covered her mouth, met my gaze and began to chuckle. I felt my belly jiggle, then my chest begin to throb. I coughed, but I couldn't control it. Auntie and I laughed and laughed and laughed.

Indian Affairs

The Leap

I DROVE IN CIRCLES looking for a free space in the underground parking lot of the office tower that housed the Vancouver office of Indian and Northern Affairs Canada. Sweaty palms and feet. I wore my new fawn-coloured Strellson suit and patterned baby-blue dress shirt, with my hair pulled back into a neat ponytail. I was as anxious as I had been at the beginning of each school year as a teacher or principal. I'd felt the same intensity leading up to combative main-table land claim negotiations: a rush of terror, excitement and virility. In the moments leading up to each session, I would find a private spot to utter a quick prayer to Mosom, my great-grandfather, to ask for strength and guidance, and it emboldened me. You never knew what would get thrown at you in treaty negotiations.

My new position at Indian Affairs carried more authority and influence, but it would clearly be less sexy. I used my old photo ID to get into the building, which like all government offices, had tighter security since the recent 9/11 terrorist attacks. On the ninth floor I wandered around until I located the large office with my name and title on the door: *Darrel J. McLeod,*

Director of Intergovernmental Affairs. The office was at the end of a long corridor, isolated from the other work stations. I chuckled. Obviously, the staff and the temporary director had designed the floor plan to keep the incoming director, me, out of sight and mind. That was fine, I thought. At age forty-three, I know a few tricks too, like management by walking about.

I had been appointed to the executive ranks of the federal government. This was considered a quantum leap for anyone, but for an Indian, even more so. There were other Indigenous executives in Indian and Northern Affairs Canada, including a Mohawk who had been the deputy minister, but the appointments still caused a stir when they happened. This was the career breakthrough I had been seeking, but I would have to prove myself to my new team and to the higher-ups in Vancouver and Ottawa. I had arrived in Vancouver just after my week-long trip to Smith to bury Trina and her cat at the foot of our mother's grave. I was mentally and emotionally depleted, but lucid enough to know I had to pull myself together for what was to come.

On my first day, I had anticipated reading a stack of briefing notes, studying a budget spreadsheet and attending bilateral meetings with the four program managers who now reported to me. Instead, my ample desktop was bare and my computerized calendar empty. The suite of offices was silent. I went looking for my new executive assistant, Manminder. The sound of muffled voices down the hall. She must be there.

Gorgeous fabric streamed through the air: fuchsia, radish red and parakeet green, lofting upward and then back down into the cardboard boxes the saris had been pulled from. Ten or more women with raven-black hair prattled energetically in what I assumed was Punjabi. Hands with elaborate gold rings grabbed and then caught and folded sari after sari, setting some off to one side. Bare cement walls. Overhead, exposed metallic bowels.

Manminder was in the middle of the melee. I called her name, trying to pronounce it correctly by gently rolling the *R* at the end. She responded in kind, rolling the two *R*s in the middle of my name. "Oh Darrel, you are here," she said. "I thought you would show up later in the day. I will be right there. I just have to finish up with the ladies and the saris."

Fifteen minutes later, she stepped into my office, looking slightly frazzled. Salmon-coloured lips stood out against the brown of her delicate, angular face. "My god, those ladies are intense. Each wants to find the most stylish saris. They are very competitive." Her voice had a lilting rhythm. When she issued a glockenspiel giggle, I felt a dumb smile take over my face. How would I tell her that the storage room sari sale had to go?

Before I could speak, she continued, "We have a great team here in IGA, you know. We provide support to the director general's office for everything that is not treaty related: education, child and family services, income support, disabilities, economic development and consultation on environmental issues. It is ver-*ry* challenging, but we have fun."

"Thank you, Manminder-*r*. I learned a lot about the directorate when I was preparing for the job interview, but I look forward to meeting the team and discussing the files first-hand."

I wasn't sure how to interpret the quizzical look she gave me in response. As Manminder stood to leave, a slim male shadow inched up to the wall of frosted glass behind her. The man pressed his hands and torso against the large window and began writhing. He forced his pursed lips against the pane, then pressed his tongue against it too, reminding me of the overgrown sucker fish in the fresh-water aquarium I'd had as a teenager. A crescendo in Manminder's giggle before she sputtered loudly, "Oh don't mind *him*. It's just *Ed*, being *crazy*."

She pulled open my office door and called out, "Ed, have you met Darrel, our new director?"

"Oh, geez, sorry, sir. Didn't see you there. Manminder here has this effect on me. She makes me crazy. I'm your policy advisor on the intergalactic files. Ha ha ha."

The man was about my height with oily strawberry-blond hair that swept back into a striated wave. He extended a pallid hand. Closely trimmed nails, index and middle fingers yellow from cigarette smoke. I had been warned about this fellow by the colleague who had encouraged me to apply for the job. "Ed's a bit off the wall," she had cautioned. "But he does good work. I hope you'll give him a chance to prove himself."

What was that dog smell? I held my breath, looked him in the eye and shook his hand. "Good to meet you, Ed."

A short woman with wire-rimmed glasses, caked-on makeup and pink lip gloss waffled up beside Ed. "Oh, I see you've met Ed. I'm Marla, Ed's manager, among other things."

"Oh, *I* can't be managed. You know that, Marla," Ed said with a Machiavellian smirk. Marla rolled her eyes and gave me a look that made it clear she thought she and I were in a different class from Ed.

"I should warn you, sir," said Ed, looking serious for a moment. "We're about three months behind in responding to ministerial dockets. They throw too much at us. S'crazy. And we go for quality, not quantity. No worries, though. I'm on good terms with the minister's assistant. He was a drummer in a band before he came to work in government. Cool guy. My personal priority is the Spotted Lake file."

"Thanks, Ed. You'll have to excuse me. I have a teleconference I'm supposed to log in to now."

Money Money Money

When I got back from lunch that afternoon, there was a single sheet of paper on my desk. A tiny yellow plastic arrow with the words *sign here* stood out from the print. What was this? I sat down to study the small paragraph of text at the bottom of the page. It was the authorization to release over a million dollars to complete the conversion of a former residential school into a hotel and casino.

I couldn't imagine a damaging institution like an Indian residential school as a resort, but upon visiting the site for the grand opening months later, I thought the transformation of St. Eugene Mission into a Delta hotel and casino had worked. When I stepped into a downstairs washroom during the familiarization tour and saw the original porcelain urinals, the hair on my neck stood on end, though, and that night, I had an uneasy sleep.

A few mornings later, two cheery economic development officers appeared at the doorway to my office carrying documents related to another project they had worked up with a First Nation. It was still my first week in my new role, and something in their manner told me I was being put to the test. Two names anyone who had lived in BC over the previous ten years would have recognized figured prominently on the pages: H.V. and K.U., a former cabinet minister in the BC government and his new wife, a former MLA. H.V. and K.U. were now, among other things, consultants for a First Nation in the central interior of BC. I perused the financial summary for the project and quickly saw that, if approved, 80 per cent of the project funds would have gone to the two former politicians, some eighty thousand dollars for a project that would last less than a year and that I assumed they would do off the sides of their desks. On my instructions the officers reworked the budget and resubmitted the forms through Manminder. I held my nose and signed to indicate approval.

The following week an even more problematic project landed on my desk. This time there was a short briefing note attached, explaining the request for hundreds of thousands of dollars to launch a new winery in the Okanagan. The project summary sounded great, a surefire success, and it had received approval in principle by my bosses. But since I held the signing authority for the funds, I had to review and approve the initiative. Intuitively, I knew something was wrong, but I didn't have the knowledge or experience to figure out what it was. I sent the proposal to a lawyer friend who was an expert in corporate law in the Department of Justice for an off-the-record review, and within a half-hour she called me.

"This initiative is set up as a joint venture under a numbered company, but a fifth grader, in ten minutes, could trace it to Senator X and Indian Chief Y," she said, sounding exasperated. "The proposal application form and the funding transfer instrument each have a clause stating that no member of the Senate, nor any elected official of an Indian band, should benefit from federal funding. What were they thinking?"

By the time we got off the phone, I was clenching my toes in my new Rockports. Senator X and Chief Y were both high-profile public figures viewed as outstanding community leaders—movers and shakers in the economic development field. They were also good friends with my boss, K.Y. I asked Manminder to book me an urgent meeting with him.

The executive floor was K.Y.'s pride and joy, with floor-to-ceiling windows, high-end office furniture and a stunning view of the twin peaks the local Squamish tribe called *Ch'ich'iyúy Elxwíkn*, meaning "twin sisters." In the late 1800s, a colonial judge had renamed them the Lions Couchant. When planning meetings with chiefs, I would book them on that floor so the chiefs could see for themselves the incongruity of the situation. They were usually speechless at the opulence, but not surprised.

I entered the suite of executive offices and saw that K.Y.'s office door was closed. V.R., the associate deputy general, second in command, ushered me into her ample office. The chic armchair and loveseat beckoned me, but she didn't ask me to sit, so we had our discussion standing up.

"K.Y. might be a while. S.M. is in his office again. As you know, he's decided to appoint her the new director of human resources. They seem to be spending a lot of time together," she said with a wink, confident I would have heard the gossip about K.Y. and S.M. I had.

"Well, let's get started. I'll fill K.Y. in, if he doesn't come along soon," continued V.R. After my summary of the situation, she stared at me.

"I don't see what the problem is. This project will bring employment and financial benefits to two communities, the senator's and the chief's."

When K.Y. entered the room, V.R. regurgitated what I had told her and repeated her conclusions emphatically.

I gulped. "Yes, but the project could also make Senator X and Chief Y very rich, and once word gets out that they accepted funds inappropriately, there will be a scandal."

My boss's pink face flushed a deep scarlet. "I pay you to come to me with solutions, not problems. You'd best find an answer I will like if you want your performance bonus this year."

As I skulked out of the executive suite, a man carrying a case of Lagavulin Scotch brushed past me. I held the door open for him and watched as he slid the box under a desk.

I was still within my first month on the job when Manminder sent me to a meeting with an architect to discuss the relocation and refurbishing of our suite of offices. We were scheduled to move from the ninth to the tenth floor of the building. The preppy architect toured me through our new location and its existing set-up before unfurling the blueprint of a new floor plan onto a vacant desk.

"Why is this happening?" I asked the young man, flabbergasted. "The office tower was built to specifications for our department just a couple of years ago, and all the furniture is new. We won't need much renovation to our new space, and we can keep the existing furniture."

"As you know, we've just completed the new executive floor," the architect said. "The director general has decided the other sixteen floors of the building should be renovated and refurbished as well. Oh, and here's the best part: you get to have his former office. It's huge, as you know, with a stunning view of Coal Harbour and Grouse Mountain. And you get to keep his cherrywood furniture and multimedia equipment."

Two months later I moved into my new office, one of the nicest in the building. I recalled the tiny combined office and staff room I'd had in the dilapidated schoolhouse in Yekooche when I was the principal there. I thought about Tl'azt'en First Nation and the many other First Nations whose offices were located in mouldy ATCO trailers and whose substandard schools on Indian reserves didn't have playgrounds or gyms. Yet for months, our four hundred or so employees had been abuzz about the million-dollar high-tech executive boardroom with its monstrous oval table, remote-control blinds, state-of-the-art sound system and giant projector with a screen that descended from the ceiling at the push of a button.

The Portrait

Friday afternoons, I could hardly wait to get into my car to race to the Tsawwassen ferry terminal, en route to my home west of Sooke. Before merging into Vancouver's rush-hour traffic, I would pop a Cree language cassette from Blue Quills College into the car stereo and turn up the volume. I had finally progressed from individual nouns and verbs to complete sentences. The rich alto of the elder's voice coming through the speakers reminded me of my *cucuum* and my aunties' voices: "*Namoya awiyak mosoyas ota otinak.*" I was thrilled that I could pronounce the sentence well, and I knew what it meant: "Here in the city we don't have any moose meat." Talk about high relevance. The last *mosoyas* I had seen was the frozen batch my cousin Maryann had gifted me a year earlier when I was home for a summer visit. She had given me what some would call moose cutlets, breaded and slowly cooked in a tangy tomato sauce. I had savoured the *mosoyas* every night for a week, knowing it might be years before I tasted it again.

One weekend at home, my distant cousin George Littlechild delivered a portrait he had painted of me. He was a very successful artist, and I had been flattered when he said he wanted me to pose for him. I'd been giddy as he adjusted my posture: "Chin up a little"; "Rotate your head slightly away"; "Remember, I'm capturing your profile." The portrait of me was to be typical of his bold, pop-style painting, and I liked his initial sketch. He had exaggerated my cheekbone, given me a hooked nose and a dramatic ponytail. With these tweaks I looked even more Cree, and that thrilled me. But when he unveiled the final portrait, I was perplexed by an object he had added to the painting—an apple sitting on the corner of a table. It looked as if the apple had initially been red, then glossed over with textured gold acrylic. He had painted the words *The Man with the Golden Apple* in a curvy script above my likeness.

I hung the painting in my house alongside several other origi-nals I had purchased from him over the years. But I was perturbed. Had George intended to give me the message that I was an "apple" Indian—red on the outside and white on the inside—and then glossed it over?

The Secret

One mid-winter morning I arrived at work at seven o'clock as usual to get a jump-start on the day. The view from my window was a dark and rainy cityscape that would remain that way for months, causing depression due to light deprivation for many Vancouverites. I put on a pot of coffee and then straggled down the long hallway to my office. A thick file folder with a blood-red

SECRET label sat on my desk. What was it, and why would anyone leave a classified document out in plain view like that?

Linda S., the manager of Child and Family Services, stepped into my office, closed the door and sat down in the chair beside my desk. She rarely came to me seeking advice or approval. "It appears we have another early bird on our team. You beat me to the coffee maker the last few days. You like it strong, I see," she said with a cautious smile, then added, "I need your final sign-off to close a case, a horrible incident involving a child in care who died on reserve. The stepfather has been charged with murder. I had to give you the whole file, but you shouldn't read it. It's macabre."

"I'll have a look at it, Linda."

"I really recommend that you don't."

I regarded her closely, suspecting that each delicate wrinkle on her determined Secwepemc face held the secret of some trauma she had deftly handled to avoid bringing scandal to the Department of Indian Affairs. We weren't paying her enough to carry that burden. After she left, I perused the file. Was somebody trying to hide something? Was there an attempted cover-up here? As I opened the folder, the hair on the back of my neck began to tingle, and I got goosebumps all over. I saw documents titled POLICE REPORT and CORONER'S REPORT, and though it went against everything I believed in, I closed the folder without reading them and signed.

The Fake Poor

I shifted my attention to the four boxes of files a slightly more senior executive member had dropped off in my office. He had been fired, forced into retirement for boldly challenging my boss, and I was to take over the work he had been doing on the oil and gas file. Ironically, this was a man who, five years earlier, had refused to begin a meeting with my team and me when I was still a novice treaty negotiator. "Nobody told me an Indian was going to be here," he had snarled, storming out of the room before the chief federal negotiator could tell him I was part of the team. Now it was 2002, and the newly formed provincial government was lobbying to have a federal moratorium on offshore oil exploration lifted as a way to bring BC back into prosperity. As a result, the oil and gas file had taken on a new importance.

Gordon Campbell was the newly elected premier of the province, and it seemed he hated not only Aboriginal people but poor people in general. While still leader of the opposition, he had tried to have the Nisga'a Treaty, which had been over a hundred years in the making, declared unconstitutional. Now, as premier, he was in the odd position of suing himself in a bid to kill a deal he was legally obliged to implement. He had also taken dramatic steps to curb social assistance to the needy, including people with disabilities. BC residents could now receive welfare for only two years out of any five-year period. That in itself was of concern, but the part that disturbed me most was this: for a family to be eligible for social assistance, at least one applicant in that family must have been employed for at least two consecutive years. In addition, applicants nineteen years of age or older were required to be independent for two years after leaving their parents' or guardians' home.

The Campbell government had proceeded to make these cuts despite public outcry and the threat of lawsuits by anti-poverty groups. Since INAC's mandate from the Treasury Board of Canada was to match provincial welfare rates and eligibility requirements on reserves, it appeared I would have to implement a policy that, from one day to the next, would cut hundreds of First Nations individuals and families in BC off social assistance. I knew this was unethical and likely unlawful. People who were already margin-alized, with little opportunity for employment in either urban settings or rural reserves, would be pushed deeper into poverty.

Federal social assistance on reserves was administered by individual First Nations or tribal councils, so we would also be putting local leaders and program administrators in the position of having to cut off their neighbours and, in some cases, family members from the meagre financial support they had been receiving.

For weeks, I received daily emails from K.Y., pressuring me to implement the welfare reforms. "There are many welfare fraudsters out there, including on reserve," he growled at me during one terse phone conversation, without providing any evidence of this. After a series of intense meetings with senior treasury board analysts in Ottawa, I sent K.Y. an email to inform him I had received permission from our treasury board representatives to delay the implementation of the new BC policy in order to consult with experts and First Nations leaders with the proviso that I come up with an appropriate plan within a year. His reply, which read something like, "Excuse me. You are going to take a year to *think* about it?" triggered countless nights of tossing and turning. How long would I be able to hold him off, and what would be the consequences of his wrath? Oh, the irony of it all—that with my childhood background of poverty and years of reliance on the welfare system for food, shelter, clothing and school supplies, I would be the one to implement these draconian measures. I thought about other members of my family, like Trina, who had relied on social assistance to complete high school and become a nurse, and my younger sisters, who as single mothers had received social assistance until they were able to get steady employment and become self-sufficient.

The Feast

I rehearsed the speaking points for the PowerPoint presentation my team had prepared for the annual spring executive retreat, trying to anticipate the questions the eight other regional executives might ask. They were known to be shark-like, and I had sparred with a couple of them while I was a treaty negotiator, challenging the entrenched status quo.

The two-day event began with a group dinner at Il Terrazzo, Victoria's premier Italian restaurant. An unobtrusive entryway from a back alley led to a stunning great room of wood and glass, with an impressive wine vault off to one side. As the waiters set platters of antipasti on our large oval table, my mouth began to water, and I struggled not to reveal how awestruck I was. Marinated portobellos and eggplant, surrounded by a ring of Caprese salad; seared scallops and smoked ahi tuna on kelp; tiny rolls of carpaccio on arugula leaves; thickly shaved curls of parmesan. I sat beside the soon-to-retire director of human resources, an Italian Canadian woman who had been very supportive in my career advancement. She had personally chosen the antipasti, and everyone congratulated her on her selection. Similarly, she had selected the wines: Valpolicella followed by Sangiovese. With dinner, we had a choice of blood-red Chianti or golden Soave. My selection was the rack of lamb, and I felt conspicuous ordering the most expensive menu item. Would everyone think I was showing off?

I couldn't believe that I was dining with these accomplished people in this exclusive place. Had I finally arrived, eluded the trap of poverty and become a successful, empowered Cree professional, as I had dreamed? The chiefs I invited to lunch and dinner meetings, the other Indigenous professionals I befriended, my family and my longstanding friends all seemed to think so. But none of them knew about my secret life, the addiction to sex that was destroying my joy and keeping alive the fear that, like Mother, I would tumble into a downward spiral and lose everything. If outed, would I end up taking my own life, like Debbie, Travis and Trina had?

I mellowed with the wine, the candlelight and the gentle smoke from the wood-fired oven. But after a final course of tiramisu with espresso and grappa, the reality began to settle in about how much this dinner would cost. Each of us must have surpassed the treasury board allowance per person for dinner after the first course and its wine pairing. I estimated my share would be at least two hundred dollars, which on my personal budget was exorbitant.

Just as the bill for the table was presented to K.Y., a friend of mine walked past. He had been my co-op student in a previous job, and he was with a man I had met before, the chief of his community. I went over to greet them. As we were shaking hands, K.Y. called out that I should invite the two of them to join us for a drink. They shook K.Y.'s hand too, and chatted politely for a moment, but didn't stay. Even so, once they were out of earshot, K.Y. leaned over to K.F., the director of corporate services, and instructed, "Note their names. We just had a business meeting with a chief. Now we can claim dinner as a hospitality expense. Thank you, Darrel." I squirmed in my seat, but our boss sat tall, pronouncing with a Cheshire Cat grin, "See you all bright and early tomorrow. I hope you enjoyed the lovely dinner—courtesy of Her Majesty."

Strike Three

My job was all consuming, but a crisis with my long-time friend Ted demanded my attention. Somehow I had enough presence of mind to make time for him and his partner, Yolande, in the evenings after the daily frenetic pace at the office.

One summer afternoon Yolande called to invite me to join them for dinner at their favourite tapas place, saying she and Ted had some important news to share. After dinner, Yolande took one of Ted's hands in hers and launched in. The day before, she said, Ted had met with his doctor and received a diagnosis of non–small cell carcinoma of the lung. I was devastated—I'd lost both of my parents to cancer, then my close friend Shirley Joseph.

Now it was my wonderful friend Ted who was dying. I struggled to contain my grief as he told me how he'd be undergoing surgery, followed by radiation and chemotherapy.

The Premier

One day an email from K.Y. flashed across my computer screen, informing me that months earlier a former premier, N.I., had received fifty thousand dollars to develop a tourism strategy for coastal First Nations. Now N.I. had requested a second grant, of an equal amount, to complete the project.

N.I. was a premier I had liked and respected. I was enthusiastic about the initiative, knowing there was great potential in the field of tourism for First Nations in BC, especially along the coast. Some nations were already tapping into it. But when the economic development team briefed me on the project's progress to date, I learned that the terms of reference were very loose, and that the single deliverable for the first grant—a coastal tourism strategy—hadn't been received. I called N.I.'s office to say we needed to see the report.

A week or so later, we received a poorly written document that simply concluded more research was required before a tourism strategy could be finalized. I was reluctant to provide more funds but knew I likely had no choice. In any case, there was a glitch, since the limit for untendered contracts was twenty thousand dollars. To their credit, my economic development team came up with a solution—N.I. could partner with an Aboriginal organization and we could flow the funds through it. After a brief conversation by phone, N.I. agreed, and we set up a meeting.

The former premier opened the meeting by launching into a long-winded discourse. When he stopped, I turned to the president of the Aboriginal tourism organization and said, "I guess it's your turn, my friend. We'd like to hear from you."

"Well, to be honest," the president responded, "it's the first time I'm hearing about this proposed partnership. Unfortunately, I can't see any meaningful role for my organization other than acting as a flow-through, and we don't do that anymore."

N.I. turned red, came over to shake my hand and left. The next day K.Y. forwarded an email he had received from N.I. It read: "One of your officials sandbagged me yesterday, K, and I am not impressed." K.Y.'s covering note to me was simply: "??????????????????!!!!" I suspected my performance bonus had just gone out the window.

The Vortex

One afternoon, near the end of the day, I got a call from my friend Lori, the DOJ lawyer I had asked to look into the proposal by the chief and the senator. "Listen, I have good news," she said. "I spoke to a colleague in Ottawa who is legal counsel for the Senate. He specializes in conflicts of interest. My colleague put in a low-key call to Senator X, and the senator has decided to quietly withdraw his proposal."

A week or so later, K.Y.'s office announced a special executive planning session, but without sending out an agenda. Was K.Y. leaving, I wondered, as had been rumoured? Instead, it turned out that the purpose of the meeting was to seek approval from the executive committee to remove economic development from my portfolio and create a separate new directorate, effective immediately. The justification was that I had far too much on my plate and the minister was planning to ramp up economic development funding.

Many weeknights and Sunday afternoons during my third year of working in Vancouver, I took a reprieve from poring over policy, budgets and briefing notes to seek out intimacy with strangers, convincing myself it would relieve my stress. Each time, like a drug, those few moments of frenzied bliss brought mind-numbing relief for a few hours. But every other waking moment, I was overwhelmed with angst and dread. I was working for a corrupt boss within a broken federal institution, the Department of Indian Affairs. How could I extract myself from that situation and keep my career intact? I had also become convinced that the RCMP or the Vancouver police were monitoring my behaviour and reporting it to the government. My irrational paranoia was fuelled, in part, by the weekly intelligence briefings on First Nations communities and individuals the department got from the RCMP.

One evening, back in my stark temporary apartment after a gruelling day at work and a perplexing evening of searching for sex, I caught my reflection in the bathroom mirror. What I saw alarmed me. The wrinkles on my forehead had deepened, and my gaze looked weary. Any trace of bright-eyed joy was gone. The combined *frénésie* of my job and my double life was pushing me out of control. I was still running four times a week and working out at the gym, but I needed more. I spent hours scanning the internet for clinical psychologists. I met with one in Victoria, but I didn't understand his approach or like his manner. Continuing my research, I came across an article about comedian David Granirer, a Vancouver counsellor, stand-up comic and keynote speaker on mental health. Apparently David's theory was that comedy was an effective way of addressing mental health issues, and he was teaching a course in stand-up comedy at Langara College. I signed up.

David got us sketching comedy bits and performing them during the first class. My attempt drew laughter. Lots of it. "You're in the zone, keep going!" my peers shouted. David lectured us about what hard work comedy was—it could take ten hours of writing to get a ten-minute act. Famous comedians like Bob Hope or Phyllis Diller had entire teams writing for them, he warned. And you had to be sensitive. White males could not make jokes about women or minorities, nor skinny people about obese people, nor the rich about the poor. The safest thing to do was to make fun of yourself.

Now I had three things to keep me from falling asleep at night: welfare reform on Indian reserves; the unpleasant possibility of helping to prepare the way for new offshore oil and gas exploration on the West Coast; and the demanding homework assignments for the comedy course. Late each evening, after I got home from the office or a quick dinner with a friend, I would sketch out new comedy bits, but the punchlines always came to me as I was about to drift to sleep. I got up to jot down the funny lines before they dissipated. The next morning, the lucidity that came with rest led me to nix most of my late-night jokes, but the ones I kept got hearty laughter and eager applause in the comedy class. By the end of our eight-week course, I had developed a ten-minute routine to use for my debut at a club on Commercial Drive.

I was pleasantly surprised by my calm as the other wannabe comedians got up and did their shtick, but as I shuffled onto the stage for my routine and spotted the faces of Ted and Yolande, a few well-known chiefs and one of my team members from the office, my knees were wobbly. I grasped the mic in one hand, gripped my tiny cheat sheet in the other and looked around me. Across the room, a waitress was chattering loudly to a table of guests who were chuckling at what she said. I called out to her. "Excuse me, my friend—should we trade places? Maybe I should be slinging the drinks and let you come up here. Whaddaya think?" That got a laugh, and then all eyes were focused on me. Could I pull this off? Would people find me funny? I zoomed in on the faces closest to me and began.

"Well, I don't know about you, but my day didn't get off to a very good start. I splashed fresh almond milk onto my Alpha-Bits, feeling self-righteous about not using dairy. They began to snap, crackle and pop. I looked down at my bowl and said, 'Hey, wrong cereal.' I stirred the Alpha-Bits anyway, until they were wet and soggy. When I stopped, swollen letters read: 'FUCK YOU, wrong *milk*.'"

Laughter.

"That left a bad taste in my mouth." More laughter.

I did a couple more bits that got applause, and then I came to the Indian proverbs, sayings from my Auntie Myrtle:

"A snip h'in time saves nine—nine more miserable brats from coming into your lives."

"Safe da pennies 'n da dollars safe themselves—then we kin go ta bingo, win real big."

The laughter was building.

"Let he among you who is wit'out sin get stoned!"

Guffaws. That last bit was a keeper.

I segued into a story about the prayer cloth I had bought for Auntie Myrtle when I visited the Vatican a few years earlier. "In St. Peter's Square, they were hawking them in all sizes, already blessed by the Pope," I said. "Small for five euros, medium for ten and large for fifteen. I didn't wanna look cheap, so I got medium. Auntie Myrtle cried when I gave it to her, back in our little hometown in northern Alberta. She and Uncle Phil had always dreamed of going to see the Pope. Auntie cherished that prayer cloth, hid it in the bathroom in its own drawer beneath the medicine cabinet. One morning, in the wee hours, Uncle went to the bathroom, still half asleep, and evacuated his bowels. I know, sounds painful, but that's the polite term for it. He reached for toilet paper and there was none. He fumbled beneath the sink—none there either. He put his hand on the sacred prayer cloth in the medicine cabinet, yanked it out, shook it open, and wiped his bum. His hemorrhoids shrank—so fast it made him pucker. He rushed out of the bathroom, struggling to hold up his pants as he told Auntie what had happened.

'Oh my god, did you flush?' Auntie asked, completely pale now.

'Jesus Christ, woman, what a question. Of course I flushed. Been a long time since we had an outhouse, eh?' Uncle retorted.

"Well, that evening Auntie Myrtle scrubbed the bathroom top to bottom, then sterilized and polished the toilet bowl with Javex until it was immaculate. She asked the priest, Father Murphy, for a gallon of holy water, then she plugged the gleaming white toilet with epoxy and filled it with the blessed liquid. Now every Sunday people come from miles around and line up outside her door to wait for a chance to kneel around the toilet in that small bathroom, dip their hands in the holy water, make the sign of the cross and pray."

"No shit!" someone yelled from the audience.

People were slapping their knees and guffawing. I was basking in the applause and hilarity, as David had taught us we should, when a squat woman with spiked grey hair and a gentle moustache, sporting a half-untucked plaid shirt, hurried onto the stage. It was Chloe, from our comedy class. When she grabbed the mic from my hand, you could have heard a feather flit. She broke the silence with a cough and, still electrified, I brushed past her to step down to the floor. She launched in. "Good evening, y'all. Well, as a former nun—yes, dear ones, I was a Sister of Charity for mor'n twenty years, o'er in Halifax. I looked e'en fun'yer back then." A slight pause for muffled laughter, then she carried on. "So, Darrel, I say this with some authority: laddie, you're gonna roast in hell."

❖

Things at work got crazier than ever, as if someone had pressed the fast-forward button on the movie that was my life. I was running on the treadmill in the basement of an Ottawa hotel the day I got a call from S.M., the director of human resources, informing me that two young women from another directorate of INAC had filed a harassment complaint against a policy analyst I'd recently seconded to my team. Next, during a routine security inspection, clerks in the mailroom came across an enlarged photo of a man's head engulfed in a vagina. The photo had been stapled to an expense claim submitted by one of my staff who worked remotely, and from the file path at the bottom of the page, the IT team determined the photo had been downloaded from the internet using a government computer. A further investigation concluded that a number of my male staff had been exchanging pornography via email while at work. The IT team purged the offensive emails from the system and issued a warning to those involved. Ed's manager had a nervous breakdown and went on short-term leave, then decided to retire. I hired an Indigenous woman to replace Marla, but days before the new woman came on force, Ed filed a harassment complaint against her—claiming that just by applying for the job she had harassed him. The director of HR decided Ed's complaint required a detailed investigation. Forms for the renewal of another employee's ten-year security clearance appeared on my desk along with the results of his criminal record check—a violent sex crime. I refused to sign. And Ted's cancer returned—a brain tumour this time.

At the annual Indian Affairs fall executive retreat in Mont-Tremblant, Quebec, clad only in the red Speedo swimsuit I had donned for the skit I produced for our team (an adaptation of the Village People song, "YMCA," the acronym changed to INAC), and emboldened by several glasses of Carménère, I rushed to the dance floor when the DJ put on salsa music. The partner I spun and dipped was a francophone deputy minister, Marie. Other costumed characters danced around us, in pairs or alone, acting up in one way or another to be comical. One very tall assistant deputy minister, disguised as a giant rabbit, hopped around eyeballing the enormous well-scrubbed carrot she held clutched between her paws.

After a few dances Marie and I chatted in French, smiling and laughing. I loved her French—it was elegant with a gentle rolling of the R and delicate diphthongs. She struck me as kind and down to earth. Before we parted ways, we exchanged *becs*. I felt a warm glow as I sauntered back to the table where my colleagues from BC were seated. But as I took my seat at the table I sensed the mood of my Anglo colleagues had shifted. When K.Y. muttered that maybe I should return to the dance floor and stay there, even my colleagues I'd thought were friends wouldn't meet my gaze. But it didn't matter—nothing could suppress my *bonheur*. It was so long since I'd had an evening of lighthearted fun and I intended to bask in it awhile.

Akikodjiwan

GLIDED ACROSS LAYERED sheets of ice, struggling to get back to my apartment hotel without falling hard on the glossy cement. Even my bulky new winter boots couldn't gain traction. "We had freezing rain late this afternoon," the drugstore clerk had explained. "It's not uncommon in Ottawa in winter and spring."

With the temperature at forty-two degrees below zero (the point at which Celsius and Fahrenheit converge—so damn cold no one cares which scale it is), I shouldn't have ventured out. But Air Canada had lost my suitcase, and the next day I was starting a new job, so I had to buy toiletries. Shoppers Drug Mart bag in hand, I shuffled along Bank Street, my cheeks and nostrils on fire, ice crystals forming on my eyelashes. With gloved hands I fumbled for my keys, pushed the door open, then trudged up three flights of stairs, hoping there was a message that my bag had been found.

I emptied the plastic bag in the apartment's sterile bathroom. Razor blades, shaving cream, toothbrush, toothpaste, deodorant, hair gel and condoms. Mission accomplished. I hoped to get a decent sleep and not be too affected by the three-hour time difference between Ottawa and Victoria. I wondered if I should call Gaylene, who was staying at my house in Sooke, having recently left her husband, or maybe Milan in Vancouver, to let someone know I had arrived safely.

❖

Akikodjiwan, the boiling rapids where the Ottawa River narrows, which the French had renamed la Chaudière, revived a terror from my childhood, when I'd dreaded crossing the long bridge with the see-through bottom that revealed the capricious current of the murky Athabasca. This cascade didn't freeze, even at forty below. The brackish water churned within a casing of ice and snow. *Akikodjiwan* must once have been an awe-inspiring natural phenomenon, but in the early 1900s it had been harnessed to generate electricity, and industrial development took shape all around it. Since then, a giant semicircular cement trap immediately below the falls had usurped their beauty and power. This sacred site of the Algonquins had never been ceded, but it had been desecrated nevertheless. Is that why I would feel such a sense of defeat whenever I saw it, a blend of resignation and impotence? Could this travesty ever be turned around?

C.D., my new director general, was a cross between Santa Claus and the Grinch, in both appearance and character. He didn't care that I had successfully dealt with the challenges thrown at me in my previous job, in the BC region of the Department of Indian Affairs: that Ed's harassment complaint had been thrown out; that after intensely arguing that any woman over the age of eighteen was fair game in his country, Esguardo, the Latino policy advisor I had seconded for a year, had taken harassment prevention training; that K.Y. had backed down on cutting First Nations residents off welfare once he saw that I was backed by both the federal treasury board and the Department of Justice in not implementing Premier Gordon Campbell's draconian welfare reform on Indian reserves; that we had convinced the relevant federal departments to fund a coordinating secretariat between the Squamish, Lil'wat, Musqueam and Tsleil-Waututh First Nations to ensure their participation in the bid phase and planning of the 2010 Vancouver Olympics; or that the offshore oil and gas panel had concluded the moratorium on drilling off the West Coast would remain in place, to perhaps be revisited in ten years. C.D. assigned me a windowless inner office and gave me every "dog" file he could find, including a new one, a no win for anyone, that would take up many of my early mornings, evenings and weekends.

INCENDIE DE LA RÉSIDENCE DU CHEF DE BANDE DE LA RÉSERVE KANESATAKE, JAMES GABRIEL was the headline of the first newspaper clipping in the bulky file folder plunked on my desk. Grand Chief James Gabriel's house had been burned to the ground after he dismissed the chief of the community police force, a man who was both a member of the community and a respected army veteran. After the grand chief fled the community with his family, a group of protestors barricaded the newly hired police chief and his constables in their station in the heart of Kanesatake. The arson and blockade had occurred in January 2004, and now, a month later, the situation remained volatile.

I worked on the Kanesatake file directly with Marie, the deputy minister I had salsa danced with at the department's executive retreat a year earlier. Long, drawn-out teleconferences in French between senior officials from the Quebec government, Indian Affairs and Public Safety Canada. Trips to the regional office in Quebec City to meet with the regional lead on the file, who consistently pronounced Kanesatake as Kanetasa*kee*, reversing the *S* and the *T* and drawing out the last syllable.

Every day for months I had to contain my exasperation as senior federal and provincial officials wrung their hands at intelligence reports from both the Sûreté du Québec and the RCMP about factions in Kanesatake being heavily armed and riding roughshod over other community members and anyone else who ventured close to the area they controlled. The decision-makers didn't dare send in the army or a SWAT team, having learned their lesson in 1990 from the experience that had been dubbed the Oka Crisis, which saw Aboriginal people from across Canada and the US stream into the area to support the Mohawk Warriors then under siege by the Canadian military. The various factions of Kanesatake—the Christians, the Catholics, the Longhouse people, the gangsters, the elders, the clan mothers and those who were just trying to live a normal life—would have to find their own solution as the politicians spied from the sidelines and tried to quietly contain the situation.

At one point, when officials from Canada and Quebec had reached agreement on an approach to policing the community, I was asked to draft a letter addressed to the Quebec minister from the federal minister. I spent a day composing it, checking the lexicon and grammar closely. I sent my final draft to the Quebec regional office of INAC for their sign off, and hours later it came back covered with red edits and a concise cover note, saying, *Nous autres, on ne parle pas comme ça.* I was taken aback at the negative reception of my efforts but made their changes nevertheless and sent the letter on to the assistant deputy minister of Public Safety Canada, a Québécois woman with a Ph.D. from the Sorbonne, for her review and sign off. Within an hour she had returned the letter with her comments: she had changed it all back to my original text. I felt vindicated, but the message from my Quebec counter-parts was clear. Being francophone was a private club that you could only be born into. Should I have told them that we might have a common French ancestor on my father's side?

His Holiness

There he was, the Dalai Lama, just feet away from me in his signa-ture maroon and saffron robes and simple eyeglasses. He was making his way around the small circle to take our hands in his and bless us. The more astute among us had brought white scarves for him to bless, but I wasn't that organized. I was back at my alma mater, UBC, to chair the President's Advisory Board on First Nations Education, a panel I had served on for eight years now. The campus was blanketed by clouds of pink cherry blossoms and multicoloured rhododendrons. What I had once considered a relatively unimportant committee had become my ray of hope in a world that felt hostile. My work life was unbearable. I was living in a bare apartment in a city I didn't like, and my sister Gaylene, with whom I'd reconciled a couple of years earlier, was living at my house and behaving strangely. When I returned to Sooke for a visit I found tiny mirrors at the base of all of the windows facing outward to keep out evil spirits and empty salmon tins scattered on the rooftop—she had tried to feed the eagles. But these scholars, deans and vice-presidents at UBC sought out my opinions and expertise.

As His Holiness moved closer, I felt tears welling up. I didn't understand why. No priest, minister or self-declared prophet from my Pentecostal days had had this effect on me. But looking at him, I realized he could have easily been Mosom Powder, my great-grandfather, to whom I looked for strength and wisdom. The humility of this man was refreshing and inspiring. How could I strive to be more like him? The next day I attended an event with the Dalai Lama and other Nobel laureates and scholars: Archbishop Desmond Tutu, Dr. Shirin Ebadi, former president of the Czech Republic Vàclav Havel, Rabbi Zalman Schachter-Shalomi and Dr. Jo-Ann Archibald. I was excited but puzzled. Why had the team at the UBC First Nations House of Learning invited me to this wondrous event? I felt so unworthy.

Back in Ottawa the following Monday I felt happy in spite of the uncertainty of my future.

Spente le Stelle

My friend Robin invited me to join him in Montreal for the weekend. It was spring, but we both had sinusitis from the prolonged cold spell that had begun in February. Robin stayed at a hotel on the English side of town, and I was at a B&B on Rue Saint-Denis. Robin showed me one of his favourite haunts, an upscale Portuguese restaurant where we shared a platter of grilled quail, chorizo and crispy octopus with *patatas bravas*, followed by dessert and the finest port I had ever tasted. We listened to a jazz quartet in a bar called Upstairs, which was in the basement of a three-storey walk-up on Mackay Street and then headed to another club to see a stand-up comedian who was a master at dealing with hecklers.

Late Saturday evening, Robin and I headed back to our respective hotels, with the tacit understanding that the night wasn't over for either of us. I wasn't sure where Robin went, but bundled up in my full-length down-filled parka, with the hood up and a wool scarf around my face, I wandered Sainte-Catherine Street until I stumbled on the gay village. The trendy look of a place called the Stock Bar drew me in. Loud music—upbeat techno. Coloured lights cutting through man-made fog created barely enough light for me to see a muscular man clad only in a Speedo swimsuit approaching me. I was convinced he was the most handsome man I had ever seen. His hairstyle was ultra-chic—who wore their hair like that? He showed me to a seat in a corner, beyond the bar, and offered to join me. Nervous and unsure of what he wanted, I lied. *"Mes amis viendront me rejoindre tantôt."* He smiled and kissed me on both cheeks before disappearing into the darkness.

Front and centre of the large open room, there was a wide stage. A tall striking man was cavorting around on it, dressed in a tight-fitting but elegant suit. He swayed and moved to the pounding beat as he enticingly removed his jacket, his suspenders and then his shirt to reveal shapely pecs. I looked around the room. This wasn't like any other place I'd been. The gay bars I had gone to in Vancouver years earlier, with Trina, Milan or friends from work, were boring and rundown, with an overwhelming ambience of sleaze. This place was clean, modern and classy. And seemingly guilt free. I was intrigued.

The stage cleared, then mesmerizing music came on. Classical sounding—a simple, steady drum beat with a molasses cello drone, then a surge of violins over a syncopated, resounding bass pattern. A silky operatic voice soaring above it all. What was this music? I had to have it. After a minute or so, a bulked-up Latino man strutted barefoot onto the stage, naked except for a skin-tight teal swimsuit that revealed an unnatural endowment. His dance was enthralling. Soon the place was abuzz with whispers, sighs and rumours. The guy next to me leaned over and said, "*Le savais-tu?—le gars est hétéro!*" The man onstage pulled off his swimsuit and continued to writhe and grind to the hypnotic music, his member swaying in the breeze of a large fan off to one side. When his slow dance was about to come to an end, I rushed to the stage exit, certain he would be swarmed as he stepped down. He appeared in his swimsuit with a towel around his neck. He shook my hand and kissed one cheek.

"*Quieres bailar conmigo bebé?*" he cooed into my ear.

"*Esta canción, amigo! Qué es? Quién la canta?*"

"*Es* 'Spente le Stelle' *de* Emma Shapplin, *que bueno que te gustó,*" he replied as he brushed past me to the next anxious fan.

The following day, at Archambault on Sainte-Catherine Street, I located the album, *Carmine Meo*. "Spente le Stelle" was the second song. I spent the blustery afternoon alone, under a comforter, with my earbuds in, directly delivering Emma Shapplin's voice. For years to come, *Carmine Meo* and Emma Shapplin's voice would travel with me wherever I went.

The Escape

Many evenings I had dinner out in Ottawa, usually in the ByWard Market with Robin, who had taken to calling me his good brother. Like many federal bureaucrats in their second year of French-language training, Robin was depressed. I gave him pep talks, offered specifics about grammar and pronunciation and taught him fancy phrases to share in class. With daily coaching, I helped him get out of the tormented situation he was in, and then he helped me out of mine. A good friend of Robin's, Bob Watts, was chief of staff to the national chief of the Assembly of First Nations. Robin reminded Bob that I had been first runner-up for the recently filled CEO job at the AFN, and they offered me the plum position of executive director of international relations. My immediate boss tried to block my secondment from Indian Affairs, as did his boss, an assistant deputy minister, but the letter went to the deputy minister for sign-off without their input.

The Friday before I began my new job, I stopped by the AFN offices to pick up the package for a conference I was to attend in Green Bay, Wisconsin, over the weekend with the leadership of the AFN and some wealthy American tribes. After checking in with the receptionist, I took a flight of stairs up one floor and located the closet-sized office I had been assigned. A file folder marked *Green Bay Economic Development Conference* lay on a desk with a chipped and worn surface. As I sat down in the swivel chair in my new office, I noticed that it leaned to one side. I understood. I would have to prove myself and earn respect in this new work environment.

I waited for Lea at an outdoor café in the ByWard Market. When she showed up, I was at once smitten and intimidated. Lea was poised, self-confident and much more accomplished than me, I was sure. She opened by saying, "Oh, Darrel, I've heard so much about you. I really hope I get to work with you. I'm glad you accepted my invitation to lunch." After a bit of probing, I learned that Lea had a master's degree in leadership, a degree in French, was a Cordon Bleu chef and had been chief of staff to the national chief during his first term in office. We conversed non-stop for over an hour at lunch that day and although the conversation was very amicable, I knew that the national chief had devised this meeting and that I would have to hire Lea, even though I didn't have a budget for her salary—I didn't in fact have a budget for anything.

Cowboys and Indians

I sat in a tiny internet café in Paris trying to get the spreadsheet formulas right. In addition to my international work, I'd taken on the AFN education portfolio as a favour to the CEO and wanted to give it my best effort. Knowing how the federal government did its fiscal planning, I didn't think it made sense for the AFN to submit a proposal for a single year of funding for a national education program. I'd sketched out a five-year plan instead, illustrating how funding could expand incrementally in elementary and secondary education and post-secondary education, and build capacity for First Nations educational administration, second-level services and infrastructure. The AFN policy team loved it. I'd heard back from them the morning of my flight to Paris, and that sunny afternoon I worked frantically to get the final details out of the way. I had two free days to explore Paris before I was scheduled to meet up with Treaty 6 chief and former Conservative MP Willie Littlechild and drive with him to Geneva, where I would coordinate the AFN delegation to the UN working group on the Declaration on the Rights of Indigenous Peoples in my primary role as executive director of international affairs.

At nine the next morning, I stood alone in the Louvre in front of the *Mona Lisa*, engrossed in the painting. An hour later, standing transfixed in the same spot, I got swarmed. Someone began elbowing me from behind. I turned my head and there was a petite Asian woman, her crooked elbow raised at a thirty-degree angle. She had decided it was time for me to move on.

That afternoon I set out on a self-directed walking tour of the city's historic, pedestrian-only streets. I got only as far as the Panthéon. It had been built as a church, then converted to a secular mausoleum for French intellectuals. After studying Foucault's pendulum, located under the great dome, I wandered down to the catacombs. For hours, the smell and feel of death wafted around me as I sought out the tombs of Jean-Paul Sartre, Jean-Jacques Rousseau and Voltaire. A surge of emotion took me aback. What was going on? This was the antithesis of my reaction at the Vatican years earlier, where I'd felt raw anger at the opulence. In the Panthéon, I felt I was in the presence of greatness—of authors and thinkers who had opened my mind and spirit and freed me from religious indoctrination.

The next day I took the métro to the outskirts of Paris, then a train to Euro Disney. I was astonished to learn Willie Littlechild had a long-term lease on a condominium within the compound there. Willie had a surprise for me and a couple of delegates from other Canadian NGOs also on their way to Geneva: he had already purchased our tickets. It was surreal wandering the grounds of the amusement park and seeing Goofy, Baloo, Mickey Mouse and Peter Pan amidst model houses with white picket fences so close to Paris.

Hours later, I found myself riding at breakneck speed with the others in a covered horse-drawn carriage, then in the middle of a pretend cowboy and Indian shootout. The "Indians" were real—young Cree men from Hobbema—and that was Willie's connection with the place. Disney had an arrangement to import the young men to be in the show and apparently gave them good benefits. I wasn't amused.

The next morning, as we drove to Geneva, Willie brought me up to speed on the long history of the UN working group on the Declaration on the Rights of Indigenous Peoples (UNDRIP). It had been established in 1982 in response to a study by a UN special rapporteur who documented the systemic oppression, marginalization and exploitation of Indigenous peoples around the world, including in affluent Western countries. The first draft of the declaration had been submitted in 1994 for UN approval, but the redrafting and approval process went at a glacial pace because of concerns expressed by states about core provisions of the draft declaration, in particular the right to self-determination of Indigenous peoples and control over natural resources on their traditional lands.

In 1995 a new working group had been established with the hope the declaration would be adopted by the UN General Assembly within the International Decade of the World's Indigenous Peoples. When that didn't happen, the working group's mandate was extended by the UN Commission on Human Rights into the Second International Decade of the World's Indigenous Peoples. Throughout the process, Canada had aligned itself with Australia and New Zealand in an intransigent troika that effectively blocked progress and caused tremendous frustration for the Indigenous participants and other states that were more progressive in their approach to human rights. In the end these three countries would vote as a bloc against UNDRIP, the approved declaration, only to end up reversing their positions over time due to pressure.

Chief Littlechild had been involved in the process almost the entire time, as had his nemesis, Wayne Lord, the man leading the Canadian government delegation. As we drove into the core of Geneva, Willie listed off the names of strong allies I should seek out and get to know: Mililani Trask, Paul Joffe, Romeo Saganash, Paul Chartrand and others.

When we arrived at a drab, nondescript building across from the secure UN compound, I joined the long, slow-moving lineup to get UN credentials. It was like a reunion—delegates who'd been involved almost as long as Willie were greeting each other with handshakes and smiles. Everyone was casually dressed, as was I, but ahead of me in the lineup I noticed a heavy-set man with braided hair wearing an expensive-looking three-piece suit. When he turned to look in my direction and called out my name, I recognized him: it was D, who was heading up the AFN delegation as the national chief's representative. At his side was a strikingly pale little person wearing a wide-brimmed ten-gallon cowboy hat.

I'd been warned I would have to manage D. In a previous session he'd made an intervention that brought embarrassment and controversy to the AFN; the national chief had had to issue a letter retracting D's statement. Would his pale friend also ask to speak in the session? The relaxed mood I'd settled into in Paris quickly dissipated.

The salon was a huge amphitheatre with small desks arranged in endless concentric semicircles that extended from one side to the other. The lighting was dim with a yellow hue. A constant shuffle of people coming and going and the persistent buzz of whispered conversation. The stagnant air took on the fragrance of each person that passed by—leather, musk, palmarosa, geranium. Each desk had a set of headphones and a dial to choose the language you wanted to hear: French, English, Spanish or Portuguese. On the stage at the bottom of the theatre behind a large table sat the chairperson of the session and his secretariat. I realized I could only hear what was going on by using headphones. I sat well behind D and the little person, ready to leap to my feet in the event either of them pushed the button on his desk to request to speak. If this happened I would rush over to discuss the content of his intervention before the chair gave him the floor. If I could help it, this would be the last time this situation would occur. From now on, someone credible and qualified, either a chief or a well-briefed expert, would speak on behalf of the AFN.

Willie had another surprise planned. He had told me we were going on an adventure after the session that day, and that I should bring a bathing suit or comfortable shorts and a towel. We drove for about a half-hour into a rural area outside of Geneva. Sturdy sunflower plants created an undulating sea of cheery yellow as far as the eye could see. When we arrived at what seemed to be a cross between a farm and a ranch, we were greeted by a man wearing a beaded buckskin vest with fringes. His straw-blond hair had been pulled back and tightly woven into two thick braids. He smelled of smoke, and I would soon see why.

The Swiss wannabe-Nehiyaw led us to a sweat lodge. In front of it several elders sat around a fire with a pile of rocks in the middle. Ah, these were the Nehiyaw elders Willie said his organization had brought over from Hobbema, I thought. I moved from one elder to the other, nodding, smiling and extending my hand.

The tallest elder, Gordon, handed me a drum and motioned for me to sit with them. I kept the beat well and did my best to anticipate the melody of their chants. The ceremony must have taken two hours in all. I can't explain what happened to me that evening, and it wasn't my first sweat lodge ceremony, but the experience was life changing. I was near tears the whole time, including during the simple meal afterward, when the banter was light and the laughter gentle. I joined the conversation in my tentative Cree, recalling the vocabulary and phrases I'd learned from Mother or on my own.

I awoke the next the morning ready to take on the world. A men's drum group convened in a large hall in the Palace of Nations prior to the meeting of the Indigenous caucus, and when one of the leaders motioned for me to join their circle, I got a shiver. I hadn't anticipated this kind of validation as an Indigenous man—a Nehiyaw—at the UN in Geneva, and here it was, happening again.

Hope

In 1996, Finance Minister Paul Martin, with Cabinet approval, had placed a cap on program funding increases for First Nations in education, social services, child and family protection, housing—all of the social programs. On paper, the federal government would still appear to be maintaining its legal and fiduciary obligation to fund these programs, but no matter how fast the population grew, and in spite of the ever-increasing costs of program delivery, funding would only be increased by 2 per cent in any fiscal year. The situation was appalling. The inequity in funding for First Nations was already huge and it was growing each year in direct proportion to inflation, the actual costs of program delivery and population growth. This, while the shocking tragedy of school-aged children committing suicide on Indian reserves gained national attention. An eight-year-old boy had taken his own life in northern Manitoba, and there were similar depressing reports from other regions.

Each day I worked on First Nations education policy, taking direction from the AFN Chiefs' Committee and its team of technical advisors, I was mindful of the situation I had encountered in Yekooche, where, for decades, the Department of Indian Affairs had delivered education in a building that had been condemned by provincial building inspectors, with substandard teachers and educational materials and no library, gym or home ec room. There was no funding for special needs assessment or special education, and we'd had to deal with several students with fetal alcohol syndrome without expert support.

I was horrified to contemplate the impact the government's funding cap would have over time on First Nations children, families and communities. Early results from a joint AFN/INAC study showed that during the five years it had been in place, the funding gap between First Nations' schools and provincially funded schools had already widened significantly.

Imposing the cap was truly a sly and Machiavellian measure of which most Canadians were not aware. At best it was immoral—at worst, it was illegal discrimination against the most impoverished and vulnerable people in the country. When Paul Martin, as leader of the Liberal Party of Canada, was elected prime minister, I was sure he would see the injustice of the funding cap he himself had put in place years earlier as finance minister—and remove it.

Early in his term, Prime Minister Paul Martin became emphatic about improving the lives of First Nations people and he developed a close working relationship with Q.G., the national chief. What began as a process of informal discussions resulted in a complex Indigenous-led initiative focused on improving housing, water, health, education, negotiations and accountability with the intent of bridging the quality of life gap between Indigenous Canadians and the rest of the population. The media dubbed the initiative the Kelowna Accord because of the planned location for the final announcement.

But for me, this translated into tedious meetings with politically correct but intransigent bureaucrats who sought to minimize the prime minister's political commitment. I recognized their strategy—wait out the ambitious politician to the end of his term; in the meantime, preserve the status quo. As the AFN's ED of international relations, I also logged countless hours of travel to Geneva, New York, Washington, DC, and Buenos Aires, either as head of a delegation or as a solo combatant, trying to advance the rights of Indigenous peoples in Canada and the rest of the Americas. I was being stretched in what felt like impossible ways.

Maelstroms

"What do you mean First Nations need funding for school board offices? Nobody has ever said anything about a budget for capital expenses," an acting assistant deputy minister growled at me. It was G.F., a heartless ringer INAC had brought in to play hardball and lower expectations. He sat across from me in the dimly lit meeting room, which was filled with a mix of exasperated Indigenous education experts, senior provincial functionaries who clearly didn't want to be there and an array of self-aggrandizing federal officials from the Privy Council Office and Indian Affairs.

"Well," I said, "if we're talking about establishing school board–like agencies for First Nations, what are they supposed to operate out of—ATCO trailers, like so many band administrations have for decades, or virtual offices? And then there are the school buildings themselves. We all know they are woefully inadequate throughout the country—only on a few select Indian reserves will you find a school building that meets the standards and codes of any province in Canada. And by the way, why is there no such thing as an assessment leading up to kindergarten entry for children with learning disabilities or special needs on reserves? No standardized testing at any level or permanent record cards?" The school principal in me was coming out.

"Capital funding is not part of the Kelowna Accord. And you know very well that special needs funding is a discussion for another day. You need to check with your leadership to get clear on what we are doing here and what we're not," the same assistant deputy minister answered in a condescending tone.

"My job is to make sure we build systems that are viable— that we set up First Nations school districts for success. For the sake of moving ahead today, I'll address capital funding in another forum, but it *will* be dealt with. My team at the AFN is studying the issue—researching how many schools across the country have libraries, gymnasiums, science labs or even playgrounds, not to mention adequate space for conducting classes. INAC officials have that information at their fingertips but choose to ignore it. Meeting provincial standards of education with respect to facilities and program funding should simply be the starting point for the federal government."

"Study it all you want—there is no capital funding within the Kelowna Accord process. Let's move on."

At the morning break, I got a frantic call from a policy analyst at the AFN. "Darrel, the Canada Revenue Agency has decided that post-secondary support funding for First Nations students is taxable and is sending huge bills to students for back taxes. Some junior official made the decision and now all of CRA, INAC and DOJ are backing him up."

"That's insane. They know education funding, including post-secondary funding, is a treaty right—a commitment—and there is case law to prove it. Let's set up a meeting with the director general of education at INAC as soon as possible."

Then, on my Blackberry, an urgent email from C.X., the chief of staff to Q.G.: *The national chief won't make the education round-table event tonight—he wants you to give his speech, in response to the minister of INAC—the one you wrote for him last night. I guess it should be fresh in your mind, eh? Lol.*

I fingered a response: *That'll go over big—a staff person giving a political address in response to the minister. The deputy ministers will go ballistic.*

The reply was instant: *Too bad. The national chief wants you to do it. Oh, and Q.G. also wants you to go to a lunch meeting with Minister Pettigrew tomorrow on his behalf to discuss the planning of the Indigenous summit in Argentina.*

One day on a lunch break from morose meetings in the bowels of some dreary hotel in downtown Ottawa, I stepped into a building with a large maple leaf flag flying outside, looking for a food court. A neon sign directed me downstairs. Washrooms too, near the pharmacy. Great. I ducked in and was astonished at how enormous the place was—a long line of urinals without separators and a row of at least eight toilet stalls.

Two angels appeared to me one right after the other, like the tag team wrestlers I'd seen on TV as a kid. Both were tall and slender—early thirties, dashing, in chic business attire, Government of Canada lanyards around their necks detached from the photo IDs they'd stuffed into their pockets. On their lunch break too, I guessed, and needy like me. As I walked back to my meeting, I chuckled at the second surreptitious lover's comment as he left: "That was amazing. You know, it's like eggs benedict. You can't get it at home."

As always, the glow wore off later that day and my conscience fired up. Sex in a public washroom—what if I got caught? I was going downhill and would end up like the others in the family. I paced my apartment. I knew I shouldn't go anywhere near *Akikodjiwan* on foot, at least not alone—and I should stop looking at it when I crossed the river by car. The risk of my own suicide was greater than ever, but I couldn't tell anyone—they'd think I was crazy.

❖

Things weren't going well. I was in Fort Lauderdale to participate in a series of meetings that would lead up to the Organization of American States's General Assembly of 2005. I had spent three sunny Florida days in dark rooms listening to speech after speech, each espousing high ideals I wasn't convinced any of the national governments involved would live up to. After hours of listening to interventions from OAS member states and non-governmental organizations representing workers, feminists, religious groups and environmentalists, I'd heard no mention of Indigenous peoples, even when topics like eliminating discrimination, the right to a basic education and combatting poverty were being discussed. My singular goal became to get these representatives of government and civil society to address the rights of Indigenous peoples explicitly instead of rolling the matter into the more general topic of human rights.

To a Prairie boy, even one who'd lived on the West Coast, the landscape of Fort Lauderdale was surreal—dikes instead of streets, and docks with moored speedboats in front of luxurious houses instead of driveways. All of the workers in the resort hotel where I was staying were dark-skinned Spanish speakers—I could've been somewhere in Latin America. The vast beach was lined with open-air restaurants and bars.

I'd been enjoying a drink in a trendy bar on my third evening in paradise, chatting on the phone to Lea back at the AFN offices in Ottawa, when my Blackberry cut out. I had a deep respect for Lea's understanding of Indigenous rights in the international context and I admired her unwavering determination to advance them. Lea knew how to garner financial and political support for our work at the AFN. And we fed off of each other. When I had an idea, Lea would amplify it, turning it into something amazing, and I did the same for her. We had been discussing the comprehensive agenda she drafted for the Indigenous summit we were organizing to take place in Argentina, and I may have spoken a couple of sentences into the air before realizing our connection was lost. I held my cellphone in front of me to check the signal strength and saw that everyone else in the bar was doing the same.

"Ah, Bush has arrived," someone said. "The signal has been blocked."

Incredulous, I stepped outside. On every street corner as far as the eye could see stood an armed male security agent wearing a black bulletproof vest—earbud embedded, hand mic resting on his shoulder. I went back to my rental car and drove to the airport to pick up Chief Shawn Atleo, the AFN lead on international issues.

After the lavish reception of the night before, I had let myself sleep in, so it was 8:00 a.m. when I set out on my usual route. The streets were lined with heavily armed soldiers and security agents. I didn't have to look up to verify it; I knew there were snipers on the rooftops of the taller buildings along the route the motorcades transporting government leaders would take. When I arrived at the lot where I usually parked, I saw that a checkpoint had been set up, and around it a smattering of orange pylons.

I stopped my car at the checkpoint and glanced around—no one nearby. I waited a couple of minutes, and still nobody. I rolled down my window to listen for voices or some kind of movement, but the place was stone quiet. I removed my foot from the brake pedal, and out of nowhere appeared two security agents brandishing automatic rifles. Their bullish voices echoed each other. "Stop the car! Stop the car. Where the fuck are you going?" Two more officers appeared behind my vehicle. Now four weapons were pointed at me, and intuitively I knew the men had their fingers on the triggers. Still pointing his weapon, one of the men approached my window and commanded, "Stay in the car. Pop the trunk, pop the hood—NOW."

Panic-stricken, I put the car in park, pulled the keys from the ignition, then lifted both hands high into the air with the car key dangling. I deliberately dropped the key onto the passenger seat, hoping they would see this and understand that I was co-operating. I fumbled to locate the small levers for the trunk and hood, then yelled back, "Hey, I'm allowed to be here. I have credentials. Check my credentials!"

Two of the agents rushed to inspect the trunk and engine, then with small inverted round mirrors inspected the undercarriage of the vehicle. Once convinced I posed no threat, the man closest to my window bellowed, "Well, let's see them fucking credentials."

I grabbed the plastic-encased cards that hung around my neck and pushed them as far out the window as I could. "See? I'm allowed into senior-level meetings, including the plenary."

When I saw the man's face relax I said, "I've driven past here each morning for the last three days without a problem."

Without missing a beat, the man yelled back, "Bush is here, Bush is here! Everything's different now."

❖

Pride, resentment and inadequacy warred within me as I strode the expansive walkway of Geneva's Palace of Nations. I was back at the UN to work on the UNDRIP, this time leading the AFN delegation. There had been much to learn about the body of international law relating to Indigenous peoples and the positions taken by various states relating to the declaration, but I felt grounded and prepared thanks to Lea, Willie Littlechild, Paul Joffe, Céleste McKay and others.

As I glanced up at the vivid flags lining the walkway, I felt sad that none of them inspired pride in me. The UN member countries together ruled the world, and many of them had oppressed Indigenous peoples and usurped their lands and resources. A number of colonial powers had committed genocide, though they refused to acknowledge it. Where was the Cree flag, or where were any other Indigenous flags? The Mexican flag featured the Aztec symbol of an eagle sitting on a cactus while devouring a serpent. At least there was that, though I knew that as a people, Mexicans were of two minds about their Indigenous past—and present. Why couldn't Canada, a country that, along with four of its provinces—Saskatchewan, Manitoba, Ontario and Quebec—carried an Indigenous name, have used an Indigenous symbol on *its* flag? Could that still happen?

On the first day of the session I made my debut—my first intervention. The discussion was on Article 28, which addressed compensation to Indigenous peoples for lands, territories and resources that had been usurped. There was no time to consult legal counsel back in the office—I had to do my best to formulate AFN positions on the fly. I used the term "redistribution of wealth" in my speech, and my intervention received loud applause, forcing the chair to call for order. Afterward, an officious-looking woman stepped in front of me. Her demeanour was severe, as was her tone of voice.

"I'm the head of the US delegation to this working group. Do you have any idea how abhorrent what you have proposed is to the United States of America? The redistribution of wealth is anathema, and when we reconvene, I suggest you retract your comments."

Representing Canada, Wayne Lord had held the position of director of the Aboriginal and Circumpolar Affairs Division for as long as anyone could remember. He was a dignified Metis man, bordering on pompous, and he was set in his ways. It took just two meetings with him for me to realize he was working with instructions from a previous federal administration—likely that of Brian Mulroney—and he intended to defend that position adamantly. As a result, Canada—both through its open interventions at the sessions of the UN working group, and in quiet diplomacy behind the scenes—was blocking the progress of the UN draft Declaration on the Rights of Indigenous Peoples, siding with the New Zealand and Australian delegations. Likely this type of thing was also happening in the parallel process the Organization of American States had underway in Washington, DC.

My second intervention at the UN working group was dramatic: "The Assembly of First Nations of Canada takes great exception to the points just made by the government representative from Canada. We do not believe the stance he has taken truly represents the position of the people of Canada, nor the present government. The approach he's taken is outdated."

Silence. A direct confrontation like this was not in keeping with diplomatic decorum. What would the consequences be?

Wayne approached me after the meeting, enraged, arms flailing. He scolded me like a child for challenging the federal government openly and on the record. His political masters would follow up with mine, he bellowed, then stormed off.

Geneva's clock was six hours ahead of Ottawa's, so I waited until the afternoon to call the CEO of the AFN to fill him in. I followed up with a long email, detailing how the Department of Foreign Affairs's approach was at odds with Canada's internal approach to negotiating treaties with First Nations. That process hadn't been a notable success either, but at least we had agreements like the Nisga'a Final Agreement, the Nunavut Land Claims Agreement and the Sahtu Dene and Metis Comprehensive Land Claim Agreement, which the signatory Indigenous peoples were happy with, for the most part. The position Wayne Lord was advancing clearly ran counter to the content and spirit of those agreements—as if he didn't know they existed.

The following morning in Geneva I learned that a new drama had fired up, and some Indigenous delegates were sure the Canadian government representatives were complicit in it: the Saami Council from Norway and the Tebtebba Foundation from the Philippines had decided to break ranks with the international Indigenous caucus and submit their own redraft of the declaration. From their version, it was apparent they had conceded to a number of the state governments' key concerns, ostensibly for expediency's sake. Was the Saami Council under the thumb of the Norwegian government? Was the head of the Tebtebba Foundation, a powerful woman with a vast reputation in the international community, actually a sellout?

Members of the Indigenous caucus were outraged, including me, but most were reluctant to express their concerns openly. After consulting with my usual collaborators, I made an intervention on behalf of the AFN asking that the Saami Council and Tebtebba Foundation withdraw their proposal out of respect for the Indigenous caucus. They refused, but after many Indigenous representatives expressed their disapproval officially, the chair simply accepted the document and classified it as "information" provided by those two organizations.

A prominent BC grand chief, F.K., asked me to accompany him as a technical advisor to a meeting he had set up with Alex Himelfarb, the clerk of the Privy Council—the country's top bureaucrat and the prime minister's right-hand man. I tried my best to not be intimidated.

When the clerk asked me, in a low-key way, what I saw as the main barriers to achieving agreements in the BC treaty process, my response was predictable. The mandate was too restrictive—the land quantum, the financial aspect, the clawback of money through what was called "own-source revenue" provisions, a concept based on a false notion of First Nations having a dependency relationship with government. First Nations hated this provision and saw it as a disincentive for them to undertake significant economic development after becoming self-governing.

I pointed out that the government had backtracked on its willingness to deal meaningfully with fisheries within treaties, demanding annual contracts outside of these agreements out of fear of backlash from commercial and sports fisheries, like what they'd experienced during the negotiation of the Nisga'a Final Agreement. Then I spoke of the personalities that were involved: two white financial analysts held the purse strings and managed to thwart the mandating process with fog and reflectors. They'd completely mystified the process for calculating the values of land and cash offers for treaties through the use of artificially complex funding formulas, which they couldn't or wouldn't explain to anyone. Through this contrived complexity, along with bluffs about having a secret and direct connection to the senior ranks of the Treasury Board of Canada, they had managed to baffle and intimidate the two people heading up the Federal Treaty Negotiation Office at the time.

The clerk listened politely and scratched notes on a single sheet of paper. F.K. patted me on the shoulder as we stood to leave. "Great job, Darrel. Thanks for coming with me." I was buzzing with excitement. Would the clerk actually consider what I'd said? Would there be changes to the treaty negotiation process as a result of my intervention? (The answer became apparent in less than a year—no new treaties were announced under the Paul Martin government.)

Another day, I watched in astonishment as a chief from BC, Nathan Matthew, and a senior policy analyst from the Privy Council Office huddled over a government computer to add their nuances to the wording of the Kelowna Accord document. Until that point, it had been unheard of for anyone, let alone an Indigenous person, to gain that level of access to the hallowed halls of the PCO.

During eighteen months of consultation, national round tables, federal-provincial dialogues and public forums, I had been the AFN lead on the education portion of the historic agreement.

It was a multilateral process that for the first time ever could lead to real progress for First Nations.

The day before I was set to travel to BC for the well-publicized Kelowna Accord announcement, my friend Umit came into my office for a chat. We'd stayed in touch all those years since we met in Taché, during which time he had served as the CEO for Tl'azt'en First Nation and held a senior position in a non-governmental organization in Ottawa. I'd recruited him to work with me at the AFN as an economist, which was his primary field of training. "You know, *Erol abi*," Umit said, using his Turkish nickname for me, "they don't need all of this fanfare—this huge and expensive PR exercise. If the government would just lift the funding cap and bring federal education funding up to provincial levels, there would be much more money on the table and it would be a far greater accomplishment."

"I know, *abi*," I said, shrugging my shoulders. "The national chief and the prime minister need this high-profile event. There's an election coming for each of them—soon."

The Eagle and the Condor

MY FOOT SLIPPED sideways. A squish underfoot, and then the odour. Fresh dog shit! Please no! My right foot had definitely settled into it, on a side street just outside my run-down hotel in Recoleta, an upscale barrio of Buenos Aires. A procession of stylishly dressed Argentines streamed around me as I assessed the severity of my misfortune. I'd had the same thing happen a couple of months earlier in Paris. What was the universe trying to tell me? To slow down? To step more cautiously? Or was it trying to keep me humble, to remind me of my rural poor boy roots?

It was July 2004, and in just an hour, I was due to meet with the leaders of ONPIA, la Organización de Naciónes y Pueblos Indígenas de Argentina. Panic. I had no other shoes, and there was no time to shop for a new pair. I rushed back into the hotel. Just outside of my room, I kicked off the offensive sandal and held it up by its back strap, well in front of me. This had to be the smelliest dog crap ever—what did they feed their *mascotas* here?

Standing at the bathroom sink, I spread Colgate Three-in-One liberally over the sole with my toothbrush and decided to let it soak in. Out in the living area, I pulled my Spanish vocabulary list from my briefcase—one last chance before meeting with the Mapuche, Diaguita, Guaraní and Kolla leaders, none of whom spoke English. I'd been warned that I would struggle to communicate with them in Spanish, so the very least I could do was reinforce the business vocabulary I would need: *cumbre*—summit, *propuesta*—proposal, *presupuesto*—budget, *despacho*—office, *tierras*—lands, *derechos indígenas*—Indigenous rights and now *caca de perro.* I was ready.

The Argentine chiefs had suggested they come to my hotel that first day. Four of them, three men and one woman, crowded into my room. I was elated about meeting Indigenous leaders from the southern hemisphere—a partial fulfillment of the prophecy a revered Shuswap elder, Mary Thomas, had made in Salmon Arm years earlier when I accepted a Canada World Youth exchange student from Paraguay to work with us at the college. The eagle and the condor would one day meet up, she'd said, and this would mark a new era for Indigenous peoples in the Americas. We would regain our rightful place as stewards of Mother Nature—*la Pachamama.*

The chiefs all had dark complexions, but unlike the Mexican Indigenous people I'd met, they didn't resemble anyone I knew back home in Canada or any of my family. Smiles all around. The tallest of them was a rotund man with an unkempt salt-and-pepper beard who introduced himself first.

"*Soy* Victor Capitán. *Muy contento que vos llegáste. Encantado,*" he said as he grasped my hand and leaned in toward me. I jerked back slightly, reversing my rudeness just in time. His beard bristled against my cheek. I hoped I wasn't blushing, but I knew I was—deeply. A man had just kissed me, in front of others, and in Canada, at the AFN offices, this would be scandalous. I could just hear the associate chief of staff muttering, "What the hell—you all fags or what?"

Next, the young female chief stepped forward. She was shorter than Victor, but an inch or two taller than me. Her cheek felt soft as she, in turn, leaned in for a kiss and cheek bump. "*Soy Natalia Sarapura*," she said in a warm alto tone.

"Ah Natalia. *Mucho gusto enconocerle*," I gushed, striving to sound both sincere and calm. Natalia exuded power and authority; she was the elected chief of a regional Indigenous organization in Jujuy, as well as an elected member of the government of her northern province. She was under thirty and a single mother to boot. How did she command respect so organically and convey such authority? Maybe she came by it naturally—her father had been a high-level *cacique*.

The other two men, both named Jorge, leaned in for cheek contact one after the other. The second Jorge was much younger than the first, suave, with an air of confidence bordering on arrogance. His smile brightened the room, even with the bulky wad of something or other lumped in his brown cheek—a squirrel with its stash. I would later find out that he was a prolific chewer of coca leaves—a mild stimulant and analgesic.

"*Donde vamos a reunirnos?*" I asked, anxious to get out of the cramped room.

"*No sabemos todavía. Pero, podemos ir a desayunar por algún lado y decidir.*"

"*Donde?*"

"*No conocemos esa zona. Vos podes eligir.*"

Great, I thought. They hadn't arranged a meeting place and they were leaving it up to me to chose a place to go for breakfast. I led the group down a narrow staircase and outside, making for a nice hotel I'd passed by the evening before. Down a few steps was a restaurant—perfect, a breakfast buffet.

Everyone ordered *café cortado*, so I followed suit. It was delicious—smooth like a latte, but without the foam. After we'd gorged ourselves on the buffet, I asked the waiter if we could linger for a bit to talk. "*Si caballero*," he said, with a *sh* intead of the usual *y* sound for the *ll* consonant. Why did it melt me every time someone called me *caba-shay-ro*?

Each of the Argentine chiefs made a long and eloquent speech. Victor, the president of ONPIA, and Natalia, the vice-president, were both skilled orators, and to my pleasant surprise I understood most of what they said. They could've been describing the plight of Indigenous communities in Canada, iterating the same demands our people had been making for years: we must emerge from poverty and inequality, re-establish ownership and authority over our lands, territories and resources; we demand equal levels of funding for education and other social programs; we need to preserve our languages and cultures, eliminate youth suicide and have proper access to housing, health services and clean drinking water; too many of our children are in the care of government; our men and women are overrepresented in the prison system. My eyes misted over and I swallowed hard.

After the speeches were over, I took the older Jorge aside to ask what they'd planned for a meeting place and an agenda. I'd intuited that he was the workhorse of the group; he seemed the most practical one. His response was vague but the meaning was clear: *nada*. I checked with the young woman at the front desk to see if the hotel had a meeting room, and after a brief discussion with the manager she said in lovely lilting Spanish, "We can offer you our diplomatic suite. It has a meeting room for up to twelve people and also a kitchenette and bedroom—*puede ser su alojamiento también.*"

The dinner we shared that night (Argentines rarely eat their evening meal before 9:00 p.m.) was a meat eater's delight—beef and pork on spits slowly roasted over a wood-fired *parrilla*, a huge indoor firepit, golden chorizo with crispy skin like I'd never sampled anywhere, *chuletón*—ribeye, *lomo*—filet mignon, *costillas*—ribs, all garnished with *chimichurri casero*. The Cree carnivore in me was ecstatic. *"Muy blanda la carne, no?"* said Victor, nodding in my direction. *"La gusta?"*

"Si, me encanta!"

When I got back to my hotel room around midnight, I flopped on the sofa. Penitence and panic had set in. I had so much work to do on AFN's education file back in Ottawa, hours of preparation for a huge upcoming federal-provincial meeting on the theme, selecting experts and allies, drawing up agendas and speaking notes for the national chief—all leading up to what would become the Kelowna Accord. My education team had once been sorely inadequate—a team leader with serious addiction problems and a couple of well-meaning analysts who didn't know the issues. But now we'd hired Jared, a highly talented economist and analyst, to assist Umit, and they had found their stride. Still, the pressure on us was enormous, and here I was parading around with these chiefs in the southern hemisphere. But I felt my work here could yield something essential.

Buenos Aires: October 17, 2004

I'm back in Argentina to continue the AFN-ONPIA planning of the second Indigenous Peoples Summit of the Americas. More chiefs arrived from different parts of Argentina today, and not all of them are committed to co-hosting a large international gathering of Indigenous leaders from across the Americas. "What will it accomplish?" one skeptical chief asked. Another jumped in: "We don't have time to champion the cause of the Indigenous people from throughout the Americas—we have our own crises to deal with. Our communities are demanding results right now, not ten years from now. What is the Organization of American States anyway, and what have they ever done for our communities? What has the government of Argentina ever done for us but oppress us—attempt to eradicate us so they can usurp our lands?"

Damn! What would I have to do to bring these chiefs onside? Wait—wasn't that Victor and Natalia's role?

I understood the chiefs' frustration, and I had to admit: most chiefs in Canada likely weren't aware of the OAS or what it had done for them, if anything. And yet, I was driven—this summit, *la cumbre*, had to happen. Getting Indigenous issues onto the agenda of the heads of state for the thirty-two member countries was critical. It would be the first time Indigenous leaders got to face down their colonizers in a forum established by the colonial powers themselves. The chiefs would be on the inside at this summit, not on par with the ministers of foreign affairs, chancellors and secretaries of state, but still legitimate delegates, representing our people. We would have our own hemispheric summit in Buenos Aires two weeks before the OAS summit in Mar del Plata, and I would accompany a small delegation of chiefs to submit a document that would be on the official record—a declaration on the rights of the Indigenous peoples of the Americas.

Ottawa: October 28, 2004

Early this morning Lea came into my office, perplexed. Our transfer to ONPIA for ten thousand dollars had gone missing. The bank here traced the transfer as far as the Banco de la Nación Argentina in Buenos Aires, but even when provided with evidence of having received the money, officials of the Argentine national bank pleaded ignorance. How in the hell would we get money to ONPIA to set up their offices and co-host the summit? I spent a half hour on the phone with a senior official in the *Cancillería*, the Argentine foreign affairs ministry, who promised to look into it.

The inane conflict between CJIRA, a fledgling group of Indigenous lawyers from Argentina, and ONPIA has deepened. Hostilities blaze openly now, and these people know how to fight:

angry missives, denunciations in the international media, letters of accusation to NGOs who are potential funders, online histrionics and finally a melodramatic call for all Indigenous rights groups and grassroots organizations in the hemisphere to unite against us—the organizing committee of the second Indigenous Peoples Summit of the Americas spearheaded by me—premised on the accusation that we are puppets of the Canadian government, which is funding most aspects of the summit.

Yesterday afternoon, I had to translate a letter the indignant Indigenous lawyers wrote to Chief Shawn Atleo, the AFN lead on international issues, accusing me of corruption and incompetence. Shawn scoffed at their allegations, yet he wasn't willing to sign a strongly worded letter I had drafted for him in response; he was only willing to say he would look into their concerns. So disappointing—I've worked hard for him, and we've been friends since my treaty-negotiating days.

Ottawa: November 2, 2004

Rights and Democracy, a well-meaning Canadian NGO, has sent ten thousand dollars to CJIRA, the lawyers' group. Fuck. It's just enough money to embolden the lawyers—give them an increased sense of legitimacy and bankroll their efforts to thwart my work.

Buenos Aires: December 5, 2004

It's so great to be back in BsAs. My third visit. I felt like a local using that abbreviation. Such a vibrant place compared to Geneva, though we barely ever got to explore the city. When we weren't in UNDRIP deliberations, we were in painfully prolonged meetings of the Indigenous caucus—late afternoons and evenings, after a full day of deliberations with the state governments—and I worried too much about my reputation and that of the AFN to skip even one session. Hours and hours of people talking to hear their own voices in four official languages.

People are less affluent in Argentina, yet they seem so much happier than the Swiss. They're definitely more *caliente*. In a rare moment, I was wandering down Avenida Corrientes, the BsAs equivalent of Broadway in New York, dazzled by the shops and sights, when a striking young man selling designer perfumes caught my eye—and I caught his. We stopped in our tracks, a foot or so apart. Wavy blond hair, blue eyes—provocative smile.

"*Vos quieres checar los perfumes?*" he asked with a smirk.

"*Si, pero no aquí—mejor en mi hotel. No está lejos,*" I answered. I couldn't believe I was being so bold, or taking such a risk—inviting a complete stranger to my hotel.

"*Vayamos!*" he replied with a mischievous smile. Sweet seduction.

He was wonderfully sensual and gentle, with surprisingly few inhibitions for a "straight" man.

Buenos Aires: December 6, 2004

Today a few elders prefaced the meeting between CJIRA and ONPIA with a ceremony that began with the handing out of coca leaves. One elder asked us to hold both hands in front of us, palms up, to receive the leaves, and after he'd said a few quiet prayers he indicated we should chew the leaves and then sit quietly for a few moments in contemplation. The leaves had a calming effect, as if I'd just had a nice hot bath or drunk camomile tea.

In spite of the ceremony, things got intense quickly once the discussions began. After an hour of dramatic polemics, the two factions reached an agreement: CJIRA and ONPIA would co-operate on the planning and delivery of *la cumbre* by sharing office space, equipment and personnel with an equitable distribution of resources from the AFN and other agencies.

As the *juristas* and *caciques* stood to shake hands and congratulate each other, I escaped to the solitude of the bathroom. As I was returning, I heard a conversation between two baritone voices in the adjacent room become a shouting match. Victor leapt to his feet. The older Jorge, usually docile, was livid. "*Mira este closet que nos dan como despacho,*" he shouted as he flung his hand to one side to indicate the tiny alcove a young lawyer had told him would become ONPIA's national office. The ONPIA leaders stormed out of the room shouting, "*Bastardos. Pendejos.*"

What could I do? I slipped away without saying goodbye to anyone and ducked into a nearby *empanadería.* What would it take to make the opportunistic lawyers give up their position and co-operate with the elected political leaders? By the time I'd eaten an empanada and reached the bottom of my pint of Quilmes, I had an idea. I'd reach out to Eduardo Nieva, the vice-president of CJIRA. We seemed to have a good connection; he was more approachable than the other lawyers, far less greedy, and seemed to genuinely care about the issues. Maybe I could accompany him to his community. Surely if we were to spend a few days together, we'd find a way to cut through the nonsensical but entrenched conflict.

I headed to an internet café in San Telmo to check emails and continue my work on AFN education policy papers. There were several messages from the AFN leadership. The CEO warned, yet again, he might cancel the summit, in spite of all the effort Lea and I had put into it, and the increasing funding commitment we'd secured from government. The national chief wanted me to explain the nasty letters he was getting from a group of lawyers, in Spanish, threatening not only to boycott *la cumbre*, but to stage a large-scale protest. The chief of staff informed me it was unlikely the national chief would travel to Argentina for the summit.

Frazzled with stress, in the cool of night and the subdued frenzy of the enormous city, I wandered about the downtown core to locate a bar I'd read about.

Sixteen hours on the bus getting to Eduardo's community. We traversed at least two climatic zones before arriving in the arid zone where he lives. I was the only person who'd taken the time to visit his community, he said, and he thanked me for making the effort. Nevertheless, it was pretty clear that unless CJIRA gained complete control of *la cumbre* and all associated funding, they'd continue ramming sticks into the spokes of our planning process.

I was shocked at how poor Amaicha del Valle was. All the buildings looked temporary and ramshackle, although they'd probably existed like that for decades—wood and adobe construction. The countryside appeared sun scorched. The mountains that defined the valley reminded me of the smaller, rounded Rockies as seen from Calgary, but the foothills and valleys there were lush, not bleak like in this place. Yet, somehow, there was something mystical about Amaicha.

Eduardo's mother was petite and fragile, much older than I expected. Eduardo told me that she was a powerful shaman who could influence weather and alter people's fate. I didn't disbelieve him; after all, my mother knew how to communicate with birds, and Cree people believe the aurora borealis are spirits that can swoop down and smother you if you whistle in their presence. Thankfully, the elder seemed to like me. When Eduardo introduced us, she clasped my hand and pulled it forward until I leaned in to kiss her cheek.

Halfway through a tour of Amaicha del Valle and its surroundings, Eduardo announced we were going to cross *el río grande*. I glanced around, puzzled—had I misunderstood his Spanish? What I saw looked like a rocky riverbed with just a trickle of water. Okay, I surmised—a seasonal river.

"When do the rains start?" I asked him.

"It almost never rains here. When we're desperate, my mother stabs the earth with her sharpest and strongest knife and does a special ceremony to bring rain, but she can only do that on very rare occasions," he said.

There used to be more water in the river year-round, he explained, but it had almost completely dried up in the last decade because of the activities of a nearby mine, which existed to provide gold to the Vatican.

On our way back Eduardo and I visited the few poorly stocked local shops to purchase food for a community feast. Oiled wooden floors, basic refrigeration. Bare stucco walls. I bought ribs, steaks, kidneys and intestines: enough for a huge *parrillada*. Potatoes, vegetables and all the fresh lettuce we could find. A warm feeling welled up in my chest—I was hosting a traditional feast for an Indigenous community thousands of miles from my homeland. But late in the afternoon, when Eduardo and I left a morose session where his people recounted the horrible injustices the Spanish conquistadores and existing government had committed over the years—dispossession of lands, forced labour, a new feudal system and, worst of all, genocide—there were no signs of a feast: no smell of smoke or aroma of meat cooking.

Eduardo explained that it turned out nobody was available to cook and he hadn't managed to find a place to hold a feast, but he assured me the food wouldn't be wasted. Bone broth for supper instead, served with crusty homemade bread we ripped apart with our hands.

Jujuy and Tucumán: December 12, 2004

Eduardo convinced someone to give us a ride in the back of their pickup truck to the highway junction where the bus to Tucumán stops. I was headed north to Jujuy, to meet Natalia Sarapura and tour her territory. Eduardo's mother gave me a loaf of bread she'd baked that morning for the trip. She looked directly into my eyes as we said goodbye, then began to sob dramatically. My own sadness turned to dread: what had she seen in my eyes? My future? Or was it my past she saw, the destruction of my people and our culture, the devastation and assimilation of my extended family?

Natalia greeted me at the bus depot, accompanied by the younger Jorge. We headed directly to a new and trendy restaurant in a rustic wood building that served Andean cuisine. Natalia had invited a local folk musician named Tomas Lipán to join us there. I was fascinated with the huge jade-green cactus on the hill outside: a single ribbed stalk with multiple branches growing out of it. It must have been eight metres tall.

"*Es el cardón grande*," Natalia said and outlined how significant the giant cactus was to her people culturally and spiritually.

I chose roasted llama from the menu. Her people ate llama now, Natalia said once I'd placed my order, but didn't use to since it was their sacred animal. Only a few people still respected that. I told her about the animals Cree people typically hunt: moose, *el alce*—with meat that is dark red and flavour packed; deer meat, my favourite, tender with a more delicate game taste; and jackrabbit, which tastes like chicken but better. Bear, *el oso*, is the sacred animal of Cree people, I continued, so we aren't allowed to eat it even though others do.

Why were the Indigenous people of Tucumán so much better off than those in Amaicha del Valle? I was curious about that, but it seemed wrong to ask. When Natalia noticed the gold rings on four of my fingers, carved by Indigenous artists from the West Coast of Canada, she got emotional.

"Our men used to wear gold," she said. "Before conquest. Now all the gold mined in our territory is for export. We can't afford it."

One of Natalia's friends, Sofia, a white woman, took me to visit a museum the next morning. I was in an altered state because of the altitude and all the travel, volatile and vulnerable. Jorge gave me coca leaves to chew, and it helped a bit.

On display in the museum were human remains, those of local Indigenous people. The labels were simple: *cráneo de una campesina*; *fémur de un campesino*. I uttered a prayer, but then began to feel dizzy. I'd had a similar reaction to seeing the remains of Aztec people in the Museum of Anthropology in Mexico City. How could anybody put human remains on display—would they do that with their own family members? An atrocity happened in this place at some point in time; I could feel it. Natalia's tribe, the Kollas, had been colonized twice, first by the Incas and then by the Spanish.

Bahía Blanca: December 16, 2004

The pampas going southward were as vast and flat as those north of Buenos Aires—kilometre after kilometre of shrubs, patches of grass and other plants. They resembled the prairies of North America, but were more parched and wilder. Grazing cattle were oblivious to their eventual fate. As night set in, the scenery faded. The seats in the bus from Buenos Aires reclined, but sleep evaded me and the trip to Bahía Blanca felt interminable.

"*Bienvenidos a nuestra ruka*," said Olga Curipán, a local Mapuche leader, as she pulled me into an embrace and kissed my cheek. Victor, my travelling companion, planted a peck on her cheek and collected a kiss in return. I tried not to stare at Olga's face, her porcelain skin, pronounced cheekbones and angular jaw, gentle crow's foot wrinkles from the corners of her eyes. Her spirit seemed to embody hope, nascent after an era of paralyzing despair. Like the tribes of northern Argentina, her people too, after a long period of successful resistance, had been subjected to genocide to free up their land for exploitation.

"The *ruka* was the traditional communal lodging of the Mapuche people," Olga explained in Spanish. It was a spacious, round building with a conical ceiling and no windows. A rectangular courtyard off to one side of the *ruka* was verdant—traditional herbs along the periphery of a carpet of trimmed quack grass. I thought I spotted a mint plant. I checked for the characteristic square stem, then plucked a leaf and sniffed it. Olga said, "*Si, hermano. Yerba buena—muy sagrada para nosotros.*"

"*Para nosotros también!*" I muttered. The slightly spicy fragrance brought childhood memories of picking wild mint for my mother and Mosom, to make their precious tea.

Abundant food, simple fare for the meal I was offered: a traditional soup made with corn and the Mapuche version of bannock, I guessed—they called it *multrun*. A ceremonial fermented drink, a homebrew made from wheat, which they assured me was an important part of their culture and not strong at all.

Once everyone was seated, Victor raised his glass, then lowered it to spill a few drops onto the floor, calling out, "*Por la Pachamama.*" The rest of us followed suit.

Afterward, Olga led us around the outside of the *ruka* to see the animal figures and designs the community had painted on its walls. My upper lip began to tremble and the dam burst. These people were struggling against all odds to revive their culture and language and seemed to be hanging on to the very last thread of it—in spite of, or perhaps because of their daunting poverty.

I recalled a conversation I'd had with the first taxi driver I met in Buenos Aires and his heartless declaration after I told him I'd come to work with the country's Indigenous communities. "*Los Indios... ya no hay. Los matamos a todos,*" he declared triumphantly. I became outraged but tried not to show it. How could he say that there were no Indigenous people left in Argentina—that they had been eradicated? Weeks later, back in Ottawa, I would read about the bounty that had been placed on the heads of some tribes in Argentina in the late 1880s and early 1900s. One, the Selk'nam, whose territory was in the Tierra del Fuego, had been exterminated—the same fate as the Beothuks in Canada.

The domination and oppression of the Indigenous peoples of Argentina by the Spanish conquistadores and the colonization of the First Nations of Canada by the British followed a similar trajectory. For decades after contact, Indigenous peoples were clearly the majority in both countries, but their numbers were drastically reduced by a smallpox epidemic, making the colonization process much easier—there would be no need for "Indian Wars" like there had been in the United States. In Canada, estimates of the loss of life are as high as 90 per cent in some regions. It isn't clear what the magnitude of population reduction was in Argentina, but it allowed Spanish settlers to become feudal landlords, forcing the Indigenous population into slave-like work conditions. Later, the self-declared landlords imposed of a form of taxation in which tribes had to remit to them a share of whatever they produced. My impression was that our Indigenous cousins in Argentina were only now finding their legs and beginning the long battle for legal recognition as a people and for the restoration of their stolen lands. Youth suicide, a critical housing shortage, poverty, low educational attainment and lower life expectancy than the mainstream population define the modern-day legacy of colonization in both Argentina and Canada.

Spanish settlers in Argentina were sloppier in their usurpation of lands than the British had been in Canada, however. The Spanish failed to set up an iron-clad land registry or simply didn't bother to register title within the system. As a result, in some parts of Argentina, Río Negro in particular, Indigenous groups were taking back ownership of large tracts of land through domestic and international courts. This work was being led by three amazing lawyers, Mapuche women from Río Negro: Graciela Carriqueo, Ana Huentelaf and Nora Aravena. These women would also be instrumental in completing the declaration of the rights of Indigenous peoples of the Americas, to be presented to the ministers of foreign affairs from the state governments.

Buenos Aires: October 26, 2005

Last night we marched through the streets of Buenos Aires displaying the flags and banners of the various tribes and Indigenous organizations from all over the Americas. The multicoloured flag of the Andean tribes was as vibrant as a gay pride flag, but instead of long bands in the colours of the rainbow, it had squares—a flashy patchwork.

Victor, Jorge and a few others had obtained the approvals necessary to close down Avenida Corrientes and get police escorts. The walk was arduous down the vast streets of the city, but a spirit of triumph reigned. Afterward, there was a *posada*—a party that usually goes late into the night. I had been joined by Lea and the other members of my AFN team, Charlie, Mike and Marlene. A grand chief who represented the national chief had arrived as well.

Buenos Aires: October 27, 2005

Registration opened at eight o'clock in the morning. Two staffers from ONPIA worked alongside our team to handle all the early arrivals. Lea's take-charge approach has been exactly what we needed. Charlie was a master with technology. My executive assistant is a whiz with logistical details and we used up every ounce of his energy and patience. And Marlene, who spoke Spanish fluently, was patient and effective in convincing a reticent contractor to repair or replace faulty equipment expeditiously.

Deliberations were set to start at 10:00 a.m. By nine there was no sign of Victor, Natalia or others on the ONPIA executive, and none of them were answering their cellphones. CJIRA and the organizations aligned with them had repeated their threat to stage a protest outside of our venue and the ONPIA team were likely afraid of being drawn into an ugly confrontation. When none of the ONPIA leaders had arrived by 9:15, I sent Natalia a text message saying that if they didn't show by 9:30, we would shut down registration and cancel all events. I was surprised by my own vehemence, but I meant it.

At exactly 9:30, two taxis dropped off the ONPIA executive group. They didn't stop for the usual hug and cheek bump. Instead, they strode right past Lea and me without saying a word. The *canciller*, Argentina's minister of foreign affairs, arrived right behind them in a black limousine. By now dark-skinned people, some wearing Andean regalia, were streaming into the conference centre and picking up the hand-crafted English, Spanish, French and Portuguese delegate kits we'd prepared. A simple but lovely logo of an eagle and a condor graced the bags.

The Argentine minister made the opening comments, followed by the screening of a videotaped message from the Canadian prime minister, Paul Martin.

For the spiritual opening of the summit, elder Fred Kelly and a number of local elders led a ceremony: eagle feathers, sweetgrass, tree fungus, sage and traditional herbs from Argentina. Swirls of smoke created a thin blue cloud. An elder from northern Argentina distributed coca leaves to the circle that had formed around the elders. After I'd smudged myself and chewed some coca leaves, I returned to my chair. I was astounded to realize this day had actually come and things were working out.

For a moment I leaned back in my chair and gazed upward to the high translucent ceiling of the conference center. I got a shiver when I saw an eagle and a condor circling overhead, calm and triumphant. I let that vision sink in, then looked around the place: eight hundred or more chiefs, elders and Indigenous professionals from all over the Americas and Caribbean had gathered—with a common purpose. *Mamaskatch.*

Buenos Aires: October 30, 2005

Following the Indigenous summit we had a week to finalize the Indigenous declaration before presenting it at the fourth Summit of the Americas in Mar del Plata, and I was astonished I still had the energy and will to continue working on it. It had been infuriating trying to reach consensus on the language of the declaration during *la cumbre*: we'd had shouting matches in the meetings of the ad hoc drafting group. It had been a true free-for-all with divergent agendas at work. Nora and Ana, the Mapuche lawyers from Río Negro, were impressively dedicated, patient and astute. We worked twelve-hour days studying notes to try to be faithful to the input of leaders from all over the Americas. Once the two of them agreed on the wording of the Spanish version and conferred with Graciela by phone, I would have to make changes to the French and English versions as best I could and run the formulations by collaborating lawyers back in Canada. Then Ana, Nora and I would send out the new draft to members of the drafting group who'd agreed to continue working on the declaration with us.

Mar del Plata: November 5, 2005

It was like a war zone in Mar del Plata, the laid-back seaside resort town where the fourth Summit of the Americas was being held. Heavily armed soldiers everywhere, regular patrols by tanks and military versions of SWAT teams in black unmarked vans, snipers and sharpshooters on rooftops. Ten thousand local and national security forces made up of federal police, the *gendarmerie* and the naval prefecture. More than twenty streets in the main beach district were blockaded. Three concentric rings of chain-link fence enclosed the secure zone; residents living inside of it carried special passes that allowed them access to their homes. If any of us were to wander out of the secure area without our special passes, it would be impossible to get back in. In fact, we could be arrested or shot for even trying to enter without the proper credentials.

We'd heard that the Argentine Navy had warships positioned offshore—the whirring and *clack clack clack* of helicopters was constant. The Argentine Air Force did regular flyovers with their A-4AR Fightinghawks. Rumour had it that the US Air Force had E-3 Sentries operating from Bahía Blanca, and there was a hundred-mile no-fly zone around the city, with orders to shoot down any planes in violation. Cellphone frequencies were jammed for hours at a time.

Finally, the main event: metal detectors and a double verification of credentials at the final security checkpoint. The Argentinian deputy minister of foreign affairs sought out me and the grand chief representing the AFN to introduce us to his boss, *el canciller*. Handshakes and broad smiles—but where were Natalia and Victor? I'd made sure they'd received credentials and invitations to all the high-level functions. Had they had a change of heart? Had the dissident Indigenous lawyers gotten to them?

I had just taken my seat near the front of the huge auditorium when my cellphone rang. It was Victor—he and Natalia had been detained downstairs. The Argentine security agents wouldn't let them in, even with their credentials hanging around their necks. I was furious. How could the Argentine government forcibly exclude Indigenous leaders from their own country?

The place was now electric with anticipation at seeing some of the most powerful men and women in the world on stage together. The grand chief was exhilarated. "Is that Condoleezza Rice?" he exclaimed. "Oh my god, we're going to be just metres away from George W. Bush."

Confounded, I glared at his profile. How could he be excited about seeing politicians the rank-and-file Indigenous people I'd been meeting with for the last two years all agreed were the enemy?

Ottawa: January 24, 2006

I stood outside of Bridgehead Coffee on Bank Street, shivering in the cold and staring at the newspaper headlines in disbelief: STEPHEN HARPER GETS HIS CHANCE. The bottom had fallen out of my world and, within weeks, years of my life's work would become unravelled: Canada would vote against the Declaration on the Rights of Indigenous Peoples and stop participating in work on a similar declaration at the OAS; the Harper government would kill the Kelowna Accord (all except the residential school apology and related initiatives—the national chief and Paul Martin made sure that element would be irreversible) and the CEO of the AFN would cancel my exchange agreement with Indian Affairs. I would have to return to work in government—a minority right-wing conservative government. Late that afternoon Lea and I raised a toast to our enduring friendship and lamented the uncertain future that lay ahead.

Fly Me to the Moon

THE ELEVATOR DOOR opened. I stepped in and found myself eye to eye with the deputy minister of Indian and Northern Affairs Canada. I had met him several times in senior officials' meetings between the Assembly of First Nations and INAC. He was usually upbeat and positive, but today he looked morose. Since the election of the Harper Conservatives the mood in Ottawa was dark.

"How is the transition going?" I asked him.

"It's horrible," he said. "We briefed Cabinet on the Nisga'a Treaty and the residential school part of the Kelowna Accord. After the Justice lawyers and treasury board folks went over those two files and our other statutory obligations, Cabinet was furious. They said they will fulfill their legal oblations, but the Indians won't get one red cent more. We're in for tough times."

The bell dinged for the eleventh floor. "*Bon courage,*" I said. "I think we'll all need it."

❖

"Figure out what it is you want and put it out there. Let it be known," Michel said as he flipped back his long greying ponytail, then lit up a cigarette. We had just finished lunch at a restaurant in downtown Ottawa and were sipping our coffee. Michel was an Algonquin traditional spiritual practitioner I had met years earlier when he was en route to BC's Royal Roads University to do a traditional ceremony. At the moment, he was an acting associate assistant deputy minister in INAC, a position he would leave fairly quickly because of the department's refusal to confirm him in it permanently. We spent another half-hour commiserating: he was frustrated by his inability to secure a senior-level job, and I complained about my career being off the rails. We called for the cheque, and I went back to my cubicle in les Terrasses de la Chaudière to continue my job search.

I was stunned at the simple clarity of Michel's advice and the chord it struck with me. I didn't know what the hell I wanted anymore. The UN draft Declaration on the Rights of Indigenous Peoples on which I had spent so much time and energy over the last two years, working alongside people who had devoted decades of their lives to it, had been rejected by the new Government of Canada, bringing humiliation to all the Canadians who had driven it forward, on both the Indigenous and the government sides of the process. Based on what the deputy minister had told me, First Nations education, my other important portfolio, would be set back by at least a decade.

Under the landmark Kelowna Accord, 1.8 billion dollars of new money would have been injected into First Nations education to fund teacher training, special education and the building of administrative systems similar to those of mainstream school districts. But when the federal NDP voted with the Conservative Party in late November 2005 to defeat the Liberal government, the accord, with the exception of the residential school settlement package, was abandoned.

For the first time in my life, I was afraid to dream. Through the haze of my depression, I knew that somehow I had to get back to my refuge, my little house on the West Coast, and to the people there who loved me.

Michel's advice made me realize that I needed mental focus, and I knew one way to achieve that was a traditional fast or a cleanse. I had to keep working, so I followed the Wild Rose Cleanse for twelve days, eliminating sugar, dairy, wheat, shrimp, mushrooms and anything fermented from my diet. I ate more fish, vegetables, brown rice, quinoa and almonds. It worked. I lost ten pounds, and my mental clarity was sharp. Colleagues at work commented on the dramatic change and asked me what I had done. My situation at INAC didn't get any easier. In fact, it intensified. But my ability to cope and to move my life forward was back. I sent my CV to all of the assistant deputy ministers in the department, and within days, I had an interview with the director general of comprehensive land claims.

❖

I got the job, and suddenly there he was again—the man who had blocked my way in the inner hallway of the Vancouver Federal Treaty Office on my first day of work there, in the winter of 1997, to interrogate me.

"Who are you, and what are you doing here?" he had demanded.

"It's okay—I'm not a villain," I had replied, laughing.

His voice got louder. "I demand to know what you are doing here. What have you got in that briefcase?"

Several people had poked their heads out of their offices to see what was going on. "Ha ha ha. Oh, Bill, it's Darrel. He's legit," someone who knew me called out.

Now, almost a decade later, here he was, holding a similar position to the one I had just been assigned, chief negotiator of self-government in the Northwest Territories. He had decided to participate in my initial briefing to ensure I heard his perspective on First Nations in the North. He sat at the head of the large boardroom table, looking authoritative and official in his metallic blue suit. His team sat on one side of the table, and mine on the other.

"They're greedy. All of them. Trying to extract every dollar they can from government and industry and you know, they spend money like drunken Indians," he held forth. Blanched forehead, matching ears. When he caught the stunned look on my face and noticed that all of my team were looking at the floor, he stammered, "Ah, I meant to say drunken sailors."

"Maybe we could reframe that, Bill," I offered, trying not to show my irritation. "The Sahtu Dene people are trying to acquire adequate funding for social programs and services for their communities from revenue gained through the exploitation of the lands and resources they own under Treaty 11 and the Sahtu Dene Land Claim. People will not get rich from the deals we make with their communities."

My new post wasn't as prestigious as my previous one, and I knew many would view it as punishment for having gone to work for INAC's historical enemy, First Nations, during my time at the AFN. But I would get to see the far North and meet with the Sahtu Dene and I would be getting back into the dynamics of negotiations as chief negotiator, one of my dream jobs.

❖

"If you reject the certainty clauses we have proposed," N.K. stated, "it will take two years, or more, to come up with a new approach." N.K. was a lawyer from the Department of Justice who had been working on the Deline First Nation and other Sahtu Dene files for a number of years. She and I were seated so close to each other that I could feel her intensity. We were in Edmonton, in a meeting room that was far too large for our group. The hotel had set up one of the usual hollow squares for us. The federal team sat on one side, five of us. The team of three for the Northwest Territories was off to our left, and the Deline team—their chief negotiator, legal counsel, policy advisor and two elders—sat directly across.

An awkward silence filled the room. Palpable tension. It was my first tripartite main table session as chief negotiator, and I was mortified—this wasn't how things were supposed to go. N.K. was my legal counsel. If we were going to take a hardline position on any topic, we should have strategized in advance and considered how *I* would present it. That's how I approached things as a negotiator.

We were discussing the sensitive topic of certainty, the concept that the agreement we reached on self-government would be the full and final agreement; as such, it would be binding and could be relied upon by all, including government, First Nations, members of the public and corporations. First Nations and the human rights community had rejected the classic "cede, release and surrender" model of Aboriginal rights as draconian and oppressive, and I agreed with them. I had to speak up. I addressed the group in the most authoritative voice I could muster, trying to ratchet the anger in the room down a few notches.

"I have worked on this topic in the past and have some insights that may not have been shared with this table as of yet. Let me do some work with other colleagues in the Department of Justice and get back to you."

"Let me reiterate. It will take at least two years to find a new approach," N.K. muttered through clenched teeth, staring straight ahead.

Negotiators for the other parties wore scowls so deep I worried they might be permanent. The chief negotiator for the Northwest Territories pounded the table and was cussing under his breath. I called for a break, stood and went to speak to the chief negotiator for Deline First Nation, who was one of the smartest men I'd ever met. He was sitting beside their lawyer, a senior partner in a national law firm who had personally argued cases before the Supreme Court of Canada. I put my hand on the negotiator's back and whispered, "Don't let her get to you. I don't know why she is stonewalling on this topic, but believe me, I will find out, and we'll come back with a different approach within months."

During a federal huddle in the corridor, N.K. positioned herself directly in front of me as if to block any possible escape. My policy advisor, K, stood at her colleague's side, her eyes burning holes in my chest. Without meeting my gaze, N.K. clenched her teeth and grumbled, "Certainty is my bailiwick, not yours. And I'm telling you where things are at. There are no other options."

"I'm not new to this topic, N.K. I worked on certainty models for years in the BC treaty process, and I know the subject matter well. The clauses you've proposed set out the least progressive option by far."

"Well, it is the model that has been approved for this table, and you have no right to contradict me like that in front of the other parties. I have been leading the discussion on this topic and have been very clear what is available."

"Well, we'll have to change that, won't we?"

N.K. and K stomped off together, shaking their heads.

The following week, back in Ottawa, N.K. and her boss met with my director general, K.M., seeking to have me removed from the Sahtu files. K.M. told me later she had reminded them I was the chief negotiator, and so was within my right to ask for a new approach to certainty if the table had come to a stalemate. The following day, the director general asked me to write a paper on how certainty could work in the Deline context. It was a complex and controversial topic that had stalled many negotiation tables. The model N.K. had proposed to Deline on behalf of the DOJ was an unscrupulous attempt to diminish the existing treaty rights of the Sahtu Dene people—an attempt to close an imaginary loophole in their land claim agreement, starting with Deline. I was excited that I would get to tackle a solution.

❖

Negotiating five separate self-government agreements was demanding, but after all I had been through, it seemed easy. Each month I spent a few days in Ottawa and a week to ten days in the Northwest Territories. The rest of the time I was home on my small acreage near Sooke. After having spent years glued to a Blackberry, travelling around Canada and abroad awaiting calls from a demanding director general, the national chief's office or the AFN CEO, it was a relief. I tended my garden, planting tomatoes, zucchini, snow peas, purple sprouting broccoli, strawberries and lots of herbs. French tarragon dominated. I played piano and guitar every day I was home: George Gershwin, Duke Ellington and Herbie Hancock; Eric Clapton, Neil Young and Blue Rodeo. I canned pickles, made salsa verde and blackberry jam. Took the time to make rabbit in mole sauce, braised beef ribs, paella and ratatouille. I travelled back to Argentina for a vacation and all that I loved about Buenos Aires was the same: kind, friendly people who were also stunningly gorgeous, succulent steak with *chimichurri*, rich red wine, flavour-packed chorizo, art museums, jazz shows.

❖

I'd only been to Yellowknife once while working for the AFN but now I travelled north of the sixtieth parallel and even beyond the Arctic Circle frequently. In the summer months, the sun only sets for an hour or two each night, so there is no frank darkness— windows must be obscured by blackout curtains for sleeping. In the winter months the sun barely rises. I found the hibernal days gloomy and wondered if Northerners battled depression just weeks into the season. Temperatures can dip as low as fifty-two below zero then.

I spent hours flying in a pressurized Twin Otter, Cessna or King Air plane over the tundra in all directions, thirty thousand feet above flat treeless ground that was frozen solid. When I could, I sat in the co-pilot's seat to better observe the landscape, hoping to see herds of caribou or perhaps even muskoxen. Sometimes I would escape into a book, usually one written in Spanish. I struggled with books like Gabriel García Márquez's *Cien años de soledad*, with its vast array of characters—for two hundred years none of them die—magic realism and complex plot line, and his *Crónica de una muerte anunciada*, where the point of view shifts from person to person like a baton being passed between runners. Other books I devoured: *Las travesuras de la niña mala* by Mario Vargas Llosa, a captivating tale of a lethally intelligent and narcissistic female double agent, and *La frontera de cristal* by Carlos Fuentes, a commentary on the social stratification and hypocrisy of modern Mexican society. Reading in Spanish helped me to recall the warmth and passion of Mexico and get through days of travel in a frosty setting where I often felt like the odd man out.

I loved that the Deline Got'ine had their own prophet—Ayah. He had pronounced more than thirty prophecies for his people and was a seer for other Northerners who sought him out. A building now called the Prophet's House had been built as a Catholic church. From the outside it still looked like a church, minus the cross atop the steeple, but inside it was a comfortable gathering place with no pews. Front and centre, where one would have expected to see a crucifix, hung an enlarged photo of Prophet Ayah. The Deline Got'ine had managed to decolonize their belief system and world view.

Deline's vision for self-government, largely based on the prophet's teachings, was comprehensive and innovative, including the principle that to truly control their territory, the Deline Got'ine must govern all who lived among them in addition to almost every aspect of their own lives. But while the Sahtu Dene were gentle, kind and conciliatory, the white consultants they hired as advisors, lawyers and negotiators were often combative—complicit with each other in their disdain for government.

After a year of working closely with my legal counsel, N.K., on three of my five Sahtu Dene files, I gained her respect. She came to readily accept my comments and suggestions for amendments to the Deline Self-government Agreement and the Tulita Agreement-in-Principle.

After countless hours of debate and discussion, the DOJ working group on certainty came around to accepting the model I had recommended in my paper. The Deline negotiations were back on a solid track.

Many winter nights the sky over Yellowknife became a painter's palette, with phosphorescent lime, magenta and teal airbrushed against a backdrop of midnight blue or hollow black. Japanese couples, hoping to conceive in the magical presence of the aurora borealis, visited Yellowknife in the winter months, believing if they were successful their offspring would have fine features and be talented. Cree people believed the northern lights to be spirits of the dead who remained in the sky, trying to communicate with their living relations. Back home in Smith I had been cautious whenever I saw them, but in the far North these vibrant spirits seemed playful and friendly—seductive even.

❖

My little house in the forest was a wonderful place to heal, and I needed to heal from the trauma of my childhood and youth and the demanding, stress-filled years of my career. Acupuncture, counselling, aromatherapy, detoxifying cleanses, long runs along the beach, swimming lessons, Spanish lessons by Skype, gardening courses. Smudge ceremonies and Jacuzzi baths with mineral salts. But I still needed something more. When I came across an ad for kundalini yoga, I decided to give it a try.

I loved projecting the image of Yogi Bhajan in the front of my mind. But after a few months, when I closed my eyes at the beginning of each session to conjure the yogi, Mosom Powder was there beside him, and this comforted me. When prolonged yoga poses were hard to hold, I pictured Mosom wearing his hand-made snowshoes, walking through crusted snow at twenty below to haul the hindquarters of a moose from the woods. During some chants, spontaneous tears spilled, paired with gentle sobbing that I kept discreet. There were kriyas for releasing inner anger, for strengthening the aura, for awakening the mind and for improving the functioning of internal organs. The ancient poem "Mother's Blessing," sung by Snatam Kaur, became my mantra. I mellowed while listening to it, imagining it was my mother's voice. After my meditation, I would extend the blessing to my dearest friends and family members by projecting their images into my mind, one after the other, surrounded by white light.

> *Retoño mio, esta es la bendición de tu madre.*
> Oh my child, this is your mother's blessing.
>
> *Nunca olvides a Dios, ni un momento*
> May you never forget God (I read Mosom and Universe), even for a moment
>
> *Adorando, por siempre, al Señor del Universo*
> Worshipping forever the Lord of the universe.
>
> *Recordando a Dios, todos los errores son purificados.*
> Remembering God, all mistakes are washed away.

Y todos nuestros ancestros son acogidos y salvados.
All our ancestors are redeemed and saved.

Que el amor sea tuyo propio y tus deseos se cumplan
May love be yours and your desires fulfilled

Que la preocupación nunca te consuma.
May you never be worn by worry.

Haz de tu mente el abejorro
Let this mind of yours be the bumblebee

Y que los pies de loto de Dios sean la flor.
And let the Lotus Feet of God be the flower.

Como el gavilán encuentra la gota de lluvia, y prospera.
Like the sparrow hawk that finds a raindrop and
flourishes.

❖

My dear friend Marion was so bloated and hunched over that I didn't recognize her the spring day we bumped into each other in Bastion Square. Her complexion was grey. She stepped in front of me and put her hand on my forearm. "What, were you just going to walk right past me?"

"Marion," I gasped. "What's going on? You look terrible."

"I know. Well, they think I have osteoarthritis or something like that. I'm going for a bunch of tests. Mom has to bring me ibuprofen in bed, and an hour or so later I can get up without so much pain. We're living here in Victoria now, you know. I'm on my way to a meeting."

"I'll lend you my nutrition bible," I offered. "It's a book on healing through modern and ancient Asian nutrition. There are detailed recommendations for people suffering from autoimmune disorders."

Marion and I had met at a conference I chaired on adult literacy while I was living in Salmon Arm in the early nineties, and we had been close since then. When I was with the government of BC and she was at North Island College, we collaborated closely in the field of post-secondary education. While I was working at the Assembly of First Nations, she became chief of her community. She did impressive work in that role. She renegotiated business deals that had been bad for her First Nation and strengthened the benefits accruing to the community, using moral persuasion. We only saw each other a few times a year once she moved to Campbell River and married, but when we did connect, it was as if we had never been apart.

All the elements had been there for Marion and me to become lovers, mutual physical attraction and emotional compatibility, but I couldn't respond to her—not when we'd first met and she was single, nor when we reconnected after she'd divorced her husband for being unfaithful.

What was wrong with me? I hadn't been in any relationship for over fifteen years. A psychologist I saw recommended a book called *The Erotic Mind*. Through it I came to understand that our desires and fantasies are shaped by our early erotic experiences. The author explores methods to help individuals understand this and to some extent retrain the erotic mind—a long and difficult process, but one that works in some cases for male victims of sexual abuse. This explained my friend Derrick's attraction to obese and balding middle-aged men—he'd been abused by a Catholic priest who looked like that. Sexually, I desired young men who resembled my former brother-in-law, Rory. I wished I'd found the book earlier in life, and that people had been as open about these things in the early eighties.

On my own, I searched out Indigenous books on sexuality and gender identity. I learned that for many Indigenous cultures in North America, sexuality exists on a continuum, rather than conforming to the simplistic labels of "gay," "lesbian," "bisexual" or "hetero." I could accept the label "two-spirited," because it involved way more than just sexual orientation—there was a spiritual and mystical side to a two-spirited person's being as well. For that reason, two-spirited people were honoured and had a particular role in society.

Marion's mother took the guidance from the nutrition book seriously. She cut dairy, wheat and sugar out of their diet, and within weeks Marion felt better. She could get out of bed without taking medication. After six weeks, she was completely back to normal and was able to cancel the long course of treatment her doctors had booked.

Marion and I had dinner together at least once a week and went dancing every weekend at Swans Pub near Market Square. We both loved the place because the owner was an art collector; he displayed phenomenal West Coast Indigenous art, and there was live music every night. Marion had moved into the field of child welfare, and was now president of an agency charged with planning the devolution of child and family services authority from the provincial government to a board composed of Vancouver Island First Nations leaders. The committee had become stagnant, so Marion asked me to do some strategic planning work with them under contract. We were a dynamic team.

On one of our dinners out, I noticed that Marion was acting a bit odd and I asked her if she was in love. She got flustered, then regarded me with a piercing gaze. "You can't just ask a question like that, out of the blue! Who does that?"

I laughed. "Well, I guess that says it all, my friend. How long has this been going on?"

"Well, I'll tell you, but nobody else can know. My mother doesn't even know, for god's sake," she said, mentioning the man's name. "He's still living with his wife, but they're no longer a couple."

"Marion, he's a dog," I said, concerned.

Within a few months, incidents between Ruben and Indigenous colleagues and friends of Marion's began to occur. One day, Ruben, a proud Caucasian of Dutch descent, called me to complain that he was experiencing racism for being white. When I didn't side with him, he and Marion cut me out of their lives. But after some time had passed, Marion began sending me emails, saying in the first one, "Life is too short to hold grudges." We resumed regular contact, and one morning a phone call from Marion interrupted my piano playing.

"I'm in a clinic having X-rays, Darrel. They were checking my abdomen, but an astute technician noticed a dark spot on one of my lungs. So they've sent me to another place, and here they're going to do a CT scan and a few other things. I'm worried."

A few hours later, I was out working in the garden when the phone rang again. It was Marion, and her voice was calm. After she had asked about my day, she told me the doctors had found tumours in thirty-nine places in her body, including her lungs, spine and liver.

The following weekend Marion called me in a panic, saying she was weak and dizzy. I sought advice from my niece-in-law, an urgent care nurse, who said Marion should go straight to Emergency. Ruben had earlier counselled her not to go to the hospital, she told me, saying Emergency was for commoners— better to wait for his surgeon friend to get back to him. A few days later, when the seriousness of the situation had sunk in, Marion asked me to be her liaison with the doctors and nurses, because she, Ruben and her parents were all completely devastated. She was forty-eight, with two preteen children.

As her advocate, the only thing I asked of the doctors and nurses was good communication with Marion and her family, including regular family conferences with her primary care doctor. No more surprise tests ordered at the last minute by doctors we had never heard of. No surprises at all. They agreed, but one day early in Marion's second week in the hospital, a specialist we had never seen before in a white lab coat entered the room carrying a clipboard. The expression on his face was stern.

"You're Ms. W? Is it okay if I speak to you in front of these people?" he asked, motioning to Marion's mother and me.

"Yes. This is my mother and my good friend."

"Well, we now know the original site of your cancer. It was your lung, non–small cell carcinoma. It has spread, as you know. It will kill you."

Marion gasped and began to sob.

"We're talking weeks or months, not years. Sorry." He turned on his heel and left the room.

❖

I ran with a warm breeze at my back, then I turned and ran directly into it. The sun reflected off Banderas Bay, thousands of tiny flashlights flickering on a surface of royal-blue water. The sand squished through my toes as each foot landed. It was December, and I would run like this daily for five weeks. Margaritas, sunshine, relaxing afternoon swims, soul-warming smiles and curious gazes from cinnamon-skinned Mexicans. How long would it be before I could do this every day for the rest of my life?

I had travelled to Mexico for the first time in my early twenties to escape the death of my sister Debbie, and I'd returned almost every year since. Here I was again, on another trip to Puerto Vallarta, this time to escape the tragedy of Marion's death sentence. I so wanted to stay close by right until the end, but I couldn't. I was concerned about how she had turned everything, including her estate and the care of her children, over to Ruben, a man she had known for only a couple of years. She had signed her will in hospital but she wanted me to review it to be sure that her children and parents were provided for adequately and to confirm that Ruben had really divorced his ex-wife.

I did speak to Ruben, and his reply was curt. Marion's request had come too late—there was nothing I could do about the will or about verifying Ruben's marital status. In just a few days, her sedation for pain had doubled, and she was drifting in and out of lucidity.

I followed Marion's situation from Mexico, speaking to her on the phone a few times a week. She was always strong, facing death head-on. She had even managed to attend a ceremony the premier of BC put on in her honour. Tears flowed down my cheeks each time we spoke, but I held my voice steady. What a coward I was.

❖

Near the end of that winter, I got a call from my niece Maggie. Her mother, Gaylene, was in the hospital, in a psychiatric ward. Maggie had thought her mother was suicidal, so she and Jennifer, her sister, signed papers to have Gaylene involuntarily committed. A week later, I flew to Edmonton, and fortunately my sister was already in a better state of mind. She told me that she and the boyfriend she had been living with in Two Hills had gotten drunk every day for the last two years, and sometimes he beat her. The last time, he'd almost beaten her to death.

I spent hours with Gaylene, sitting in the psych ward or outside at different spots she had found on the well-kept grounds. She chattered non-stop and lit up cigarettes one after another while I tried to dodge the smoke. Before I left, I helped to get her into an addictions treatment program in Calgary. She was an alcoholic, not a psychiatric case.

That spring, my gardening intensified. I planted winter crops in cold frames, a made-in-Sooke version of a mini-greenhouse.

I was ecstatic to have arugula, Arctic King lettuce and radicchio year-round. My prize crop was garlic. Each year I kept the largest cloves from the grandest bulbs and planted them in October to harvest new bulbs in July. Some plants grew so thick at the base I thought they were onions that had volunteered. On the morning of my birthday I was outside harvesting garlic, gleeful about my bumper crop. That evening Milan and I were going to Markus's Wharfside Restaurant, the best restaurant in Sooke. A plump robin observed me, trilling and squawking, anxious for me to leave so he could pluck the succulent worms I had unearthed and fly them to his nest. A gentle wind stirred the alder leaves overhead, creating the usual comforting rustle.

I was absorbed in the moment when Milan's voice broke the spell. "De-rol, come to the phone. It's Jennifer's husband."

What now? I thought. They never call me unless something's up.

"Hello. Jay?"

"Hey, Uncle, sorry to bother you, but Jen asked me to call. Something's happened with Dylan."

"Really? I haven't spoken to Dylan for a while. You know, he called me a couple of times last month asking if he could come out to live here."

"I didn't know about that. Well, he attempted suicide early this morning."

"Oh, god. But he's okay, right? Is he in the hospital?"

"No, unfortunately, he passed away. He hanged himself on the headboard of his mother's bed."

I dropped the phone, numb. As I staggered into the house, memories of Dylan flashed through my mind—the fun we'd had when he was five and he insisted on making music with his older brother, Frank, and me—him pouncing on the keyboard while Frank and I played my hand drums. I grabbed one of those drums from atop the piano and went into my bedroom to do a smudge but more memories awaited me there: the times Dylan had slept in my bed as a toddler, moving in a spiral around the bed until the blankets and sheets were all twisted up in a thick braid.

I had to chant and drum right away, light sage and sweetgrass to help Dylan's spirit transition to the other side and to block the force of grief before it debilitated me. I could feel it coming on—my mind was becoming a vacuum, my chest beginning to ache. As the fragrant smoke wafted around me, I drummed and danced, letting the spirits guide me. I improvised a song, a chant similar to those I had heard Mosom sing when I was little. I prayed for Dylan's safe passage. This bought me peace—for an hour or so.

I went to the living room and sat on the red velvet wing-back chair where Dylan had loved to perch himself to watch TV. I'd failed him. He'd asked to come live with me several times in the last year, but I'd said no—I was travelling for work too much and didn't want to leave a thirteen-year-old alone in my house for weeks at a time. There might have been other ways I could have helped, but I didn't take the time to consider those—I'd wanted to avoid dealing with his mother and stepfather, who both had strong personalities.

Then I thought about Marion. I'd failed her too. I'd left Mother to die alone in a hospital, and my Wet'suwet'en friend Shirley when she died of liver cancer, even though her family told me she'd asked for me in her last moments of lucidity. The best I'd done was with my friend Ted—I'd managed to stay with him until hours before he died. Still, I wasn't there for his actual passing.

Why hadn't I helped Dylan? Then I caught myself. I realized what I was doing, assuming guilt and responsibility beyond what was reasonable. I had to pull myself together—I was going out for dinner with Milan in a few hours to celebrate my birthday. There was no way I was missing that.

My god, Dylan had killed himself on my birthday. Was he sending me a message?

I stood onstage in a classy jazz bar, overlooking palm trees that lined the beach and seawall in Puerto Vallarta. Beyond the palms was a Maya-blue ocean covered in gentle ripples. The sun had just set. I was holding a microphone, and to my left stood Rafael, the bearded guitarist who had been giving me lessons for the last two years. Behind me was Gary, a virile Mexican drummer with a provocative moustache, and beside him, Roberto, a talented bass player I had admired in a number of shows around town.

I counted them in: "*Uno... dos... tres... cuatro*," and launched into "Besame Mucho." Vigorous applause. Next, we performed our version of "Cry Me a River," followed by a bluesy song, "Forget What I Said" by Noora Noor. We ended the set with "Fly Me to the Moon," me singing the melody of the last verse up a major third. As I left the stage to get a glass of wine, both strangers and recent acquaintances approached me to shake my hand and talk.

Later that night, back in my rustic Mexican apartment, I was too charged to sleep. My dream was coming true. I was becoming a jazz singer, and it was my second full winter in Puerto Vallarta. Stephen Harper's reckless layoffs of federal workers had served me well. I had taken early retirement and paid off my mortgage in Sooke with the money from the buyout package.

My Haida friend Frank brought his family from Edmonton to Puerto Vallarta for a vacation that winter, and on their third day there, they invited me to go zip lining. Previously I had gone with my niece Jaime and her husband in Cabo Corrientes, south of Puerto Vallarta, and loved it. But on the eve of the zip line trip with Frank, I awoke in terror in the middle of the night, entangled in the simple sheet that covered me. I had dreamed about Dylan—his last visit to my house, when he was ten. He had danced around my kitchen anticipating a summer feast of all the corn on the cob, steamed new potatoes and barbecued hamburgers he could eat. Blackberry pie with ice cream for dessert.

What a shock that a happy-go-lucky thirteen-year-old would want to take his own life, and on my birthday to boot. I remembered other fun times with Dylan, hours splashing and swimming at Thetis Lake and French Beach. Images of him as a toddler, poised regally in my white kitchen sink as his mother bathed him each night of the three months they lived with me. On a summer visit when he was in Grade Three, he wrote me a note. It said, "Uncle, I'm a bad boy. I'm really bad." I should have asked him why he thought that, but I didn't. Why hadn't I found a way for him to come and stay with me when he had reached out? Why was I so afraid of risk?

My memories enthralled me. Suddenly, I was convinced that if I were to go zip lining the next day, I would join Dylan, along with my siblings who had committed suicide, Debbie, Travis and Trina. An image flashed through my mind of me pulling free of the zip line at its zenith and flying through the air into the river valley hundreds of feet below. It seemed inevitable.

During the zip line fun I'd had with my niece Jaime and her husband, I had briefly mused that this would be a phenomenal way to die. Now I was actually thinking through the mechanics of it. I would need to study the harness release carefully, so as not to botch it up. I didn't want to be injured and cause a scene or have anyone see me go through the horrible stages of dying. For the first time ever, I felt I couldn't trust myself, even though I didn't understand why I would do it. I wasn't sad, depressed or angry. I was experiencing incredible joy as a jazz singer, and I anticipated many wonderful things ahead of me—completing my first book, more music, love, travel, great food and adventure. The next day, along with the guilt of not joining in the zip line trip with Frank and his boys, I had the bittersweet feeling that I had escaped death—cheated fate, if that was possible.

As much as scientists know about suicide, one element remains elusive: in the decisive moment, what is it that drives a person to actually go through with it? After extensive research and consultations with my exceptional family doctor, I came to understand that, in addition to life's daily trials and tribulations, there are genetic, cultural and historical factors that influence a person's behaviour in powerful ways. As a survivor of what some call acculturation and others call genocide, and a survivor of systemic and individual racism, of sexual abuse and other family violence, I would have to remain vigilant for the rest of my life. I could never take a simplistic view of suicide nor back away in abhorrence when someone else mentioned it. Perhaps the only way to ensure that suicide never claimed me would be to help others to conquer its demon. It is a devil, what Mosom would have called a *maci manitou*, whose time and moment of arrival is unpredictable and always shrouded in mystery.

Kicikamis

A BIRTHDAY PARTY WITH moose nose and *kakiwak* instead of cake. Imagine. But everyone was cheery, on the edge of laughter. Mother and I were ecstatic we could all be together for my birthday, and in a foreign place for everyone but me: the West Coast, where trees were so hefty it took the outstretched arms of at least two people to hug an average-sized trunk, and the lowest branches extended thirty or forty feet. Each of those bottom branches was as big as any tree might be in the forest of northern Alberta, where we were from. Here we were, gathered at my little cabin and acreage—four of my six siblings with their children, Mother, her eight brothers and sisters and their mini-tribes of kids: Auntie Margaret and Uncle Pat with fifteen, Uncle Jack and Auntie Agnes with eleven, Auntie Rosie and Uncle Charlie with the same and Uncle Tiny and his wife and three children. Auntie Diane, sat alone in the emerald-green armchair in a black miniskirt, legs crossed and hands in a near clasp in her lap.

Presiding over it all, in their self-deprecating way, were Mosom Powder and Cucuum Philomene. Mosom's face long and slender, with a thick grey moustache, and Cucuum's the opposite, round and smooth, both with a dark-brown complexion and the deep wrinkles that come with time and tension. They were seated by the picture window, across from each other at my bulky and rustic dining table, sipping peppermint tea. All of us were mesmerized by the movement of the *kicikamis*—the Strait of Juan de Fuca, an arm of the Pacific that on this day glimmered and shifted more than ever, reflecting the azure sky and competing for attention with the snow-capped Olympic Mountains just beyond. Would we see whales—the pod of orcas that lived nearby?

Many people remarked on the abstract portrait hanging in the hallway, painted by our distant cousin George Littlechild. When I told them it was of me, they were surprised.

"Ha. Your nose isn't hooked like that; it's wider and flatter."

"Your hair was long and black then, like charcoal."

"The eyes, they're magical, follow a person aroun' the room."

"How come he called it *The Man with the Golden Apple*?"

I thought back to how concerned Mother had been a couple of days earlier. How she had turned to Mosom, who had arrived early to visit and help prepare—chop wood, snare rabbits and net fish—and said to him in Cree, "*Mah!* How the hell we gonna fit everyone in?" Mosom laughed briefly and then replied. Mother translated for me. "He thinks we're silly to worry. We'll make a big firepit out back that we can gather around—an outdoor living room like when he was young. With all this brush around here, be easy to build lean-tos. We'll find some canvas for tipis. He says ta tell 'em all ta bring sleeping bags or blankets, and maybe we could even borrow tipis from the local Nehiyawak."

Something else had occurred to her this morning. She went over to Mosom and extended a hand outward as she spoke. "*Mosom, namoya Nehiyawak ota.*" I understood most of what she said. She was clarifying something from their earlier discussion. "Nehiyawak call some of the tribes here Flatheads 'cause o' their tradition o' shaping the heads o' the babies of high-ranking family members to be more oval. They don't have tipis. They have long houses, live in family groups and have winter dances."

"*Tapwe-ci*," Cucuum Philomene answered for him. "*Napakstagwana*—those with flat heads. Would like to meet some of them. Trade moose meat for salmon."

The three of them went on to talk about how the local people must have lived. I understood enough key words to know they were pondering whether people used horses, bows and arrows, or boats and spears when hunting and fishing. What animals did they hunt, Mosom wondered aloud. And what about their *muski-kiwapoy* (medicine or tea) and their ceremonies? Were theirs only in winter? Ours were in the summer—the sweat lodge and sun dance. Did they make *kakiwak*—dry meat?

There were stories back home that some of the coastal tribes ate the flesh of their enemies, and Mosom was sure those here must have heard that our people at times ate dog meat, squirrel and beaver. I had so much to tell him. I wanted to discuss the Vancouver Island tribes I had come to know, the Nuu-chah-nulth, the Lekwungen and the Kwakwaka'wakw: their food, cultures and traditions. I knew Mosom was fascinated by the *Dzunukwa*, or wild woman of the woods mask hanging above my fireplace and the other masks, drums and paintings in the house. But I didn't want to overwhelm Mother or my uncles with having to translate so much at once. There would be time. They must have good medicines, Mosom guessed.

Mosom and I moved to the adjoining family room and sat so close on my oxblood, green and white plaid couch that our legs and shoulders touched. We didn't say a word as we watched the flames frolicking in the river-stone hearth. His familiar smell comforted me. It was different from that of the old white men I had worked with in extended care at Vancouver General. Mosom had a gentle smoky odour of pipe tobacco and Tiger Balm and the manly smell that all of my uncles had. My grown-up nephews had it, and I probably did too. The Caucasian seniors smelled of mouthwash, glycerine soap and 2-nonenal.

A few kids had gathered by the picture windows to point at something outside. A large doe and two fawns were nibbling on the gooseberries I had planned to pick the day before. Then they pointed down the driveway to where two women had opened the wide metal gate. My older sisters, Trina and Debbie, were coming up the driveway, hand in hand like when they were little. I didn't think I would ever see the two of them getting along like this, not in my lifetime, but here they were, arriving together. I was so used to playing mediator between the two of them: what would I do now? And Diane would be so happy to see Trina. They had been inseparable as kids.

Auntie Margaret took charge of the fires in the front room, in the TV room and outside. She got her oldest boys to chop wood and make kindling. My cousins, Maryann, Chiq-iq, Lah'pi and Lady, were already hard at work in my large kitchen with its bright white cupboards and grey ceramic floor, baking bannock and cutting up the *mosoyas*, onions, potatoes and carrots to make a huge pot of moose stew. I admired their beautiful brown complexions, wishing I was as dark. But my father had Scottish and French blood as well as Cree.

Uncle Jack's boys Dennis and Max were in the forest, helping my brother Travis to set up tipis for the women and build lean-tos for the men. There was bear scat around, so Mosom told them and all the other men to pee outside, on the edge of what would become our encampment, to delineate our area. "Bears are sacred and our animal guide. We're blessed to have them nearby."

When Mosom overheard a few of the boys talking about "tipi creeping" at night, he told Uncle Jack to remind them that all these girls and women were their aunties or cousins, so they'd better keep their energy for another time. If they wanted to play amongst themselves, that was their business. The young guys laughed and said it was easy for an old man to say that. Uncle Jack was halfway through translating the last bit for Mosom before he realized what he was saying. Mosom laughed and said in Cree, "Tell them if they reach my age and still wake up with a throbbing hard-on, they'll be lucky. Even the old guys who can't do it think about it and wish they could." Mosom laughed again, so heartily it caught on like wildfire. Soon we were all laughing, and some cousins went up to Mosom to shake his hand and slap his back.

Back at the house, my nephew Joseph had some reggae music blasting—Bobby McFerrin singing "Don't Worry, Be Happy." Mosom whistled along with the opening and shuffled his feet to the beat, the way he would in a tea dance: tap one foot slightly, slide it in front of the other, then shuffle the back foot forward and tap it too; repeat. Halfway into the song, he asked Mother what the words meant. He laughed—"*tapwe-ci*," then laughed some more before saying something in Cree to Cucuum Philomene. She laughed too.

❖

As the west sea breeze picked up outside, it magically conjured a wall of fog from the ocean surface and pushed it toward us, chilling the air. An unusual pigeon with a delicate white crescent around its neck landed on an elder bush covered with drying red berries and pecked away at them before flying off again. A robin splashed around in the green plastic plant tray that served as a bird bath sitting atop a hemlock stump. A raven's sombre *h'aah-aah-aah   h'aah-aah* croak in the forest. Mother, Debbie and Trina were visiting with Gaylene, who was the fairest at the house so far. Mother appeared distraught—on the verge of tears. Everyone in the room knew she was about to say something important, so they hushed.

"I feel so upset that me and my brothers, Louis, Jack 'n Andy, and our aunties, have to translate for Mosom and Cucuum because you kids can't talk Cree. 'Tso unfair. But I thought I done the right thing—you too, eh, Marg'ret—when we taught you kids English and tol' you to speak it every time you asked us about a Cree word. The nuns brainwashed us inta thinkin' our language was bad and our culture evil, 'n I fell for it. Shoulda been smarter, even tho' I was only a kid at the time. Now I see I was wrong. In just two generations we're losing our beautiful language, Nehiyaw. I still love it, and it is the language I dream in, but I see it will be impossible to bring it back in our family. Such a tragic mistake. Horrible, 'cause it ain't like Chinese, Hebrew or Swedish—all them languages got a home base. Millions of people speak them in their everyday life. They won't ever get lost. But our home territory, our vast land, was stolen and our language could be lost in twentih years and nobody cares. I feel so 'shamed o' what I done. Darrel and Trina speak some, but Debbie's kids and grandkids don't speak a word. Two generations and it's lost. Hurts so much ta' see that you kids can't talk with Mosom and Cucuum the way I done my whole life—we've always been close. How can you get close to a person if you can't even share a simple conversation or have some cultural things in common? *Wah wah sosquats.*" Mother moaned as she left the room. I went after her. "Mom, it's not your fault. They punished you. It was more like torture for a seven-year-old, bread and water for two days for speaking Cree."

Someone had moved the yellow cedar ceremonial rattle carved in the shape of an eagle's head that usually sat on a brick shelf over the wood stove. Likely Mosom. Where had he put it?

"How can you ever forgif' me, son? We were sep'rated by this barryer o' language our whole lives. Now I see it so clearly. You can' even talk to Mosom and Cucuum. Hurts so much ta' see the longing in your eyes to speak with them, go deep, and you can't."

Mosom joined us and put his arm around Mother's shoulder. "*Mahti poni mahto Ndans. Dh'on wh'orih, pee happih,*" he said.

Mother glanced at him and forced a smile. Mosom was right. What was the point in worrying? More important to pray.

When Mother and I returned to the family room, Mosom, Cucuum and a few uncles and aunties were talking. Uncle Jack translated snippets to let the rest of us in on their conversation:

"When they were young, our people were the majority, Cucuum said. It was like that for decades, so most *Moniyawak* learned Cree to trade with us and make money. Some nuns and priests spoke it really good—even wrote it down. But they brought diseases that killed so many of our people. They put a bounty on the heads of the buffalo to starve our cousins on the plains, force them onto reserves, and us too—we used to join them in hunting parties."

Mother, Auntie Margaret, Uncle Jack and the other Cree speakers nodded. We all sat in silence for a few minutes, staring down or straight ahead.

Cucuum cleared her throat, then continued. "Once the *Moniyawak* outnumbered us, they tore apart our culture one piece at a time. Outlawed powwows and gatherings, our form of government. Took our kids away when they were still really small and taught them English. Brought French-speaking nuns and priests in to teach it to them, along with their religion. They hardly spoke English and never used it between themselves. Spoke fran-saey—*wem'stigoso*. Forced us to end our seasonal migration from the northern bush to the Rocky Mountains, fed us whisky—*iskotewapoy*—'til it ruined us. A real bad dream. Too bad to be true."

She glanced around the room. "We didn't have no heaven or hell before they came, and we weren't ashamed of our own naked-ness. We enjoyed sex and talked about it freely. We didn't hide it away in darkness, and we didn't have VD—their men brought that too. We ate good—nobody was fat or had diabetes. And we knew how to laugh—a good belly laugh that healed us and kept us going."

Then, more quiet. I remembered this type of silence, when we were content just to be together and sit there happy with life.

After a while, Mosom spoke to Mother in Cree. She turned to me. "He wants you to tell us about your travels, my man. I told him that you have travelled to many places."

I didn't know where to start, so I began with the Three Sisters mountains at Canmore—how I'd marvelled at them at the age of ten. They'd become my surrogate grandmothers. Did Mosom know there were Cree names for those mountains? Then the beauty of BC. I couldn't settle on one place, so I described other Rocky and Coastal Mountains—how I loved the waterfalls that adorned them like diamond necklaces. Rivers, streams, mineral hot springs, lakes and ocean; magnificent forests of cedar and spruce. I told them how nature had healed me and given me new vigour—right there, at my little house near Sooke.

I told them about Mexico—the jungle, warm ocean, masses of cinnamon-coloured faces, mangos and coconuts, the Huichol people. During the spring and fall equinoxes the setting sun turned the shadows on the steps at Chichen Itza into an illusion of a Mayan deity, a feathered serpent, slithering down its banister. The Aztecs called that same deity Quetzalcoatl: god of wind and rain, of knowledge and learning.

I described how the Mapuche and other peoples of Argentina had welcomed me, sharing their ceremonies and feasts.

Mosom turned again to Mother, shook his head, nodded in my direction and said, "*Mah, sosquats. Peyakow.*"

"He can't believe you did all those travels alone, Son. You took our spirit to all those places—alone."

❖

The next morning after a breakfast of bannock with jam made from berries Auntie Margaret's family had picked the summer before, we got the kids outside to play Red Rover—two lines eight feet apart, facing each other. It made us aware that three out of four kids were fair, most blond with blue eyes. The contrast between them and our aunties was striking—cinnamon bark beside cream. And it wasn't just their skin. Their facial features were different, too. Joseph Junior, Debbie's son, was the only one his age with an olive complexion and prominent cheekbones. How did these kids feel seeing their great-grandparents? Did their wind-worn brown faces inspire love and pride like they had for me since I was a toddler, or did they feel shame and confusion? And what about Cucuum and Mosom? In just four generations, our language was gone and our gene pool diminished. There was no denying it when the truth was standing right before us. Their intense love for these children who were so beautiful, smart and caring, was mixed with a sense of loss. Something important was gone forever.

"Cultural genocide," the chief justice of the Supreme Court had written in a key judgment in May 2015. Her words sparked outrage in many quarters, especially for the Conservative government of the day. But many agreed with her. I knew all too well what she was talking about. I had seen it first-hand in my family, even though my people had fought against it.

That night around the fire, Mosom's eyes glowed like the projectors I'd seen at the back of old movie theatres. I knew he was up to something. At dawn the next morning I heard some noise—first a woodpecker drumming on the spruce tree outside my window, then slower rhythmic thuds. I threw on a T-shirt and shorts and went to investigate. Mosom was chopping at a large cypress tree in front of the house.

"*Kîkwâhtikowiw?*" I asked him.

"*Osi. Ninohte osi,*" he said as he swung the axe again.

Back in the house, Mother was waiting for me at the door.

"*Osi.* Mosom says he needs one. What is that?" I asked her.

"A boat. He's going to build a boat."

❖

We're floating down a river. At least I think it's a river: I can't see land in any direction. The current is swift, and our boat is moving so fast I wonder if we are out of control. Giant cedar stumps float by, and I worry that one will crash into us. Overhead, PACs buzz by. People on their way to the city to work. Such a shame they don't pool to conserve energy. I can't wait until scientists perfect the quantum teleportation device to replace these personal aviation craft.

Mosom wouldn't allow us to bring any communication modules. He had insisted that we remove the neural lace from the back of our heads. Some of us have perfected telepathy, though, and can pick up general frequencies or specific channels that way. There is a Cree channel now. It isn't perfect, but at least it uses our "Y" dialect.

Mosom has grown taller and the glow in his eyes is constant now. He can speak English even without a module in his neck. We don't know how he did it. For many, spoken language is now obsolete, since we can project our thoughts and images directly into each other's minds. But Mosom treasures the sound of the human voice.

Below deck, my aunts and uncles are sitting around a large table. I am the youngest family member Mosom allowed on the boat. Now that we can all communicate, I understand better Mosom's killer sense of humour.

"*Tanti toh'ti'hen*, Mosom?" I ask him, eager to learn more about where we are going.

"We'll know when we get there. For now, we are on this boat and here we'll stay. We have otter, beaver and muskrat on board, and they need to do their work."

Mosom won't tell me, but I know. I saw it in a dream. We are going back to our ancestral homeland in the boreal forest around James Bay, and to an earlier time—a time when we lived in harmony with the land and the animals. Joy, sadness and terror fill me to the brim.

❖

"*Wanisca nikosis*. Happy birthday." I awaken to Mother's voice. "*Wanisca*—long nap!"

Everybody is standing around my bed in my little house near T'Sou-ke. Mother and Mosom lead me to the dining room. The sky outside has brightened. A giant birthday cake covers the table—so many candles I can't count them.

"*Waseskwan*," Mother says. "It's a beautiful day."

ahpo ekosi

Acknowledgements

A T THIS STAGE of my writing career, I hardly know where to begin in terms of expressing gratitude. I owe so much to so many. Of course, I have to thank close family and friends—the living, the dead and those yet to come—for giving me the courage and inspiration to write this sequel to *Mamaskatch*. My great-grandfather, Mosom Joseph Powder, is my constant strength and guide, as are my mother, Bertha Dora, my father, Clifford James (Sonny), and my siblings Debbie, Trina and Travis. Ginger Tindell, a longstanding member of the Puerto Vallarta Writers' Group who is now in the spirit world, gave me astonishing praise and encouragement when others in the group were less convinced. RosAngelica Moreno, also of the PV writers' group, has been an unrelenting support, as has Kandace Andriadis, who scolded me about my early drafts being pedantic. (She was right.)

Joanne Mitchell, Yolande Levasseur and Jay Kerig reviewed several draft chapters as advance readers. Barbara Pulling provided astute and instructive editorial and artistic advice, as did the CEO of Milkweed Editions, Daniel Slager. Betsy Warland and Shaena Lambert continue to be wonderful mentors, as do other members of my ever-expanding family of writers, including Caroline Adderson, Jennifer Manuel and Sarah Selecky. Sarah's short-story intensive provided me with valuable techniques for varying my approach to content and structure. Eden Robinson, Esi Edugyan, Terese Mailhot, Joshua Whitehead, Louise Bernice Halfe and Bev Sellars have all been incredibly supportive of my work, and their amazing bodies of work inspire me.

Anna Comfort O'Keeffe, Corina Eberle and the rest of the team at Douglas & McIntyre have been kind, patient and incredibly enthusiastic. They've treated my work with nothing less than loving care. My agent, Carolyn Forde, has been a great force for getting my writing out into the world.

I thank José Joaquin Medina and Iván Estrada for helping manage the day-to-day operation of my household and life in Mexico, freeing me up to write, edit and write some more. Their encouragement as they observed the highs and lows of a writer's life was invaluable. Rafael Zermeño inspired me to renew my profound commitment to music, which has enriched my entire life and my writing in particular. I thank the Canada Council and the jury of the Governor General's Award for choosing my first memoir, *Mamaskatch*, as the winner of the 2018 non-fiction prize.

Milan Dobranic, my constant companion for over thirty years, remained patient as I rambled on in excitement about the various successes of *Mamaskatch* and the intense process of writing and editing *Peyakow*. He shared wise advice in response to my countless ideas and schemes, and he made sure I ate healthy dinners the days I didn't think about anything but writing.

Finally, I extend gratitude to David Evans, proprietor of the Stick in the Mud Coffee House in Sooke, for letting me hang out in his establishment to write, edit and do internet research, and to David and other good friends, patrons of the Stick, for listening to my frequent updates on *Mamaskatch* and *Peyakow*.

Peyakow

DARREL J. MCLEOD is the author of *Peyakow* and *Mamaskatch*, which received the Govenor General's Literary Award for Nonfiction. He is Cree from treaty eight territory in Northern Alberta. Before deciding to pursue writing in his retirement, McLeod was a chief negotiator of land claims for the federal government and executive director of education and international affairs with the Assembly of First Nations. He holds degrees in French literature and education from the University of British Columbia. He lives in Sooke, British Columbia.

milkweed
editions

Founded as a nonprofit organization in 1980, Milkweed Editions
is an independent publisher. Our mission is to identify, nurture
and publish transformative literature, and build an engaged
community around it.

Milkweed Editions is based in Bdé Óta Othúŋwe (Minneapolis)
within Mní Sota Makhóčhe, the traditional homeland of
the Dakhóta people. Residing here since time immemorial,
Dakhóta people still call Mní Sota Makhóčhe home, with four
federally recognized Dakhóta nations and many more Dakhóta
people residing in what is now the state of Minnesota. Due to
continued legacies of colonization, genocide, and forced removal,
generations of Dakhóta people remain disenfranchised from
their traditional homeland. Presently, Mní Sota Makhóčhe has
become a refuge and home for many Indigenous nations and
peoples, including seven federally recognized Ojibwe nations.
We humbly encourage our readers to reflect upon the historical
legacies held in the lands they occupy.

milkweed.org